YEAR B
AFTER PENTECOST 2

YEAR B
AFTER PENTECOST 2

PREACHING
THE REVISED
COMMON
LECTIONARY

Marion Soards
Thomas Dozeman
Kendall McCabe

ABINGDON PRESS
Nashville

PREACHING THE REVISED COMMON LECTIONARY
YEAR B: AFTER PENTECOST 2

Copyright © 1993 by Abingdon Press

This book is printed on recycled, acid-free paper.

Library of Congress Cataloging-in-Publication Data
(Revised for vol. 4)

Soards, Marion L., 1952–
    Preaching the revised common lectionary.

    Includes index.
    Contents: [1] Advent/Christmas/Epiphany—   —
[4]After Pentecost 2.
    1. Lectionary preaching. 2. Bible—Homiletical use.
I. Dozeman, Thomas B. II. McCabe, Kendall, 1939–
III. Common lectionary (1992). IV. Title.
BS534.5.S63   1993   251   92-36840
ISBN 0-687-33802-6 (vol. 1)
ISBN 0-687-33803-4 (vol. 2)
ISBN 0-687-33877-8 (vol. 3)
ISBN 0-687-33876-X (vol. 4)

93 94 95 96 97 98 99 00 01 02   —   10 9 8 7 6 5 4 3 2 1

MANUFACTURED IN THE UNITED STATES OF AMERICA

Contents

Introduction... 7

Why We Use the Lectionary.. 9

**PREACHING AND WORSHIP AMIDST THE
CLASH OF CALENDARS**................................. 13

Proper Seventeen—Sunday Between
August 28 and September 3 Inclusive........................... 19

Proper Eighteen—Sunday Between
September 4 and 10 Inclusive..................................... 29

Proper Nineteen—Sunday Between
September 11 and 17 Inclusive....................................39

Proper Twenty—Sunday Between
September 18 and 24 Inclusive....................................49

Proper Twenty-one—Sunday Between
September 25 and October 1 Inclusive........................... 59

Proper Twenty-two—Sunday Between
October 2 and 8 Inclusive..69

Proper Twenty-three—Sunday Between
October 9 and 15 Inclusive.. 80

Proper Twenty-four—Sunday Between
October 16 and 22 Inclusive.......................................92

Proper Twenty-five—Sunday Between
October 23 and 29 Inclusive...................................... 103

Proper Twenty-six—Sunday Between
October 30 and November 5 Inclusive........................... 114

All Saints—November 1 or the
First Sunday in November... 124

Proper Twenty-seven—Sunday Between
November 6 and 12 Inclusive..................................... 134

CONTENTS

Proper Twenty-eight—Sunday Between
   November 13 and 19 Inclusive.................................... 144
Proper Twenty-nine (Christ the King)—Sunday Between
   November 20 and 26 Inclusive.................................. 154
Thanksgiving Day.. 165

SCRIPTURE INDEX... 175

A COMPARISON OF MAJOR LECTIONARIES...................... 179

A LITURGICAL CALENDAR:
PROPER SEVENTEEN THROUGH
   CHRIST THE KING 1993–2001................................... 187

This is one volume in a twelve-volume series. Each volume contains commentary and worship suggestions for a portion of lectionary cycle A, B, or C. Since the lectionary readings for a few special days do not change from one lectionary cycle to another, material for each of these days appears in only one of the volumes. Appropriate cross references in the table of contents lead the reader to material in other volumes of the series.

Introduction

Now pastors and students have a systematic treatment of essential issues of the Christian year and Bible study for worship and proclamation based on the Revised Common Lectionary. Interpretation of the lectionary will separate into three parts: Calendar, Canon, and Celebration. A brief word of introduction will provide helpful guidelines for utilizing this resource in worship through the Christian year.

Calendar. Every season of the Christian year will be introduced with a theological interpretation of its meaning, and how it relates to the overall Christian year. This section will also include specific liturgical suggestions for the season.

Canon. The lectionary passages will be interpreted in terms of their setting, structure, and significance. First, the word *setting* is being used loosely in this commentary to include a range of different contexts in which biblical texts can be interpreted from literary setting to historical or cultic settings. Second, regardless of how the text is approached under the heading of setting, interpretation will always proceed to an analysis of the structure of the text under study. Third, under the heading of significance, central themes and motifs of the passage will be underscored to provide a theological interpretation of the text as a springboard for preaching. Thus interpretation of the lectionary passages will result in the outline on the next page.

Celebration. This section will focus on specific ways of relating the lessons to liturgical acts and/or homiletical options for the day on which they occur. How the texts have been used in the Christian tradition will sometimes be illustrated to stimulate the thinking of preachers and planners of worship services.

I. OLD TESTAMENT TEXTS

A. The Old Testament Lesson

    1. Setting

    2. Structure

    3. Significance

B. Psalm

    1. Setting

    2. Structure

    3. Significance

II. NEW TESTAMENT TEXTS

A. The Epistle

    1. Setting

    2. Structure

    3. Significance

B. The Gospel

    1. Setting

    2. Structure

    3. Significance

Why We Use the Lectionary

Although many denominations have been officially or unofficially using some form of the lectionary for many years some pastors are still unclear about where it comes from, why some lectionaries differ from denomination to denomination, and why the use of a lectionary is to be preferred to a more random sampling of scripture.

Simply put, the use of a lectionary provides a more diverse scriptural diet for God's people, and it can help protect the congregation from the whims and prejudices of the pastor and other worship planners. Faithful use of the lectionary means that preachers must deal with texts they had rather ignore, but about which the congregation may have great concern and interest. The eroticism of the Song of Solomon, or the elaborate imagery of blood and sacrifice in the letter to the Hebrews, both of which we encounter in this volume, might be cases in point. Adherence to the lectionary can be an antidote to that homiletical arrogance which says, ''I know what my people need,'' and in humility acknowledges that the Word of God to be found in scripture may speak to more needs on Sunday morning than we even know exist, when we seek to proclaim faithfully the message we have wrestled from the text.

The lectionary may also serve as a resource for liturgical content. The psalm is intended to be a response to the Old Testament lesson, and not read as a lesson itself, but beyond that the lessons may inform the content of prayers of confession, intercession, and petition. Some lessons may be adapted as affirmations of faith, as in *The United Methodist Hymnal,* nos. 887-889; the United Church of Christ's *Hymnal,* nos. 429-430; and the Presbyterian *Worshipbook,* no. 30. The ''Celebration'' entries for each day will call attention to these opportunities from time to time.

Pastors and preachers in the free-church tradition should think of the lectionary as a primary resource for preaching and worship, but need to remember that the lectionary was made for them and not they for the lectionary. The lectionary may serve as the inspiration for a separate series of lessons and sermons that will include texts not in the present edition, or having chosen one of the lessons as the basis for the day's sermon, the preacher may wish to make an independent choice of the other lessons to supplement and illustrate the primary text. The lectionary will be of most value when its use is not a cause for legalism but for inspiration.

As there are no perfect preachers, so there are no perfect lectionaries. The Revised Common Lectionary, upon which this series is based, is the result of the work of many years by the Consultation on Common Texts, and is a response to ongoing evaluation of the *Common Lectionary* (1983) by pastors and scholars from the several participating denominations. The current interest in the lectionary can be traced back to the Second Vatican Council, which ordered lectionary revision for the Roman Catholic Church:

> The treasures of the Bible are to be opened up more lavishly, so that richer fare may be provided for the faithful at the table of God's Word. In this way a more representative portion of the holy Scriptures will be read to the people over a set cycle of years. (*The Documents of Vatican II*, Walter Abbott, ed. [Piscataway, N.J.: New Century, 1974], p. 155)

The example thus set by the Roman Catholics inspired Protestants to take more seriously the place of the Bible in their services and sermons, and soon many denominations had issued their own three-year cycles, based generally on the Roman Catholic model, but with their own modifications. This explains why some discrepancies and variations appear in different forms of the lectionary. The Revised Common Lectionary (RCL) is an effort to increase agreement among the churches. A table at the end of the volume will list the differences between the RCL and the Roman Catholic, Episcopal, and Lutheran lectionaries. Where no entry is made for the latter, their use accords with the RCL.

For those unacquainted with the general pattern of the lectionary, a brief word of explanation may be helpful for sermon preparation. (1) The three years are each distinguished by one of the Synoptic

10

Gospels: Matthew in A, Mark in B, Luke in C. John is distributed over the three years with a heavy emphasis during Lent and Easter. (2) Two types of readings are used. During the periods of Advent to Epiphany and Lent to Pentecost, the readings are usually topical—that is, there is some common theme among them. During the Sundays after Epiphany and Pentecost the readings are continuous, with no necessary connection between the lessons. In the period covered by this volume, we review sections of the Wisdom material and the writings of the Old Testament, leading finally to the story of Ruth and ending with the story of Hannah, who functions as a prefiguring of Mary (Advent is approaching!) and who brings us back to the beginning of the summer when we began with the story of God's call to her son Samuel. The New Testament lessons are a review of the letters of James and Hebrews, and in the Gospel readings we continue through the Markan narrative. There are no intentional thematic connections between these readings, but the preacher is provided with a rich source of material each Sunday to relate to the life of the congregation. The difficulty will be to decide which lesson upon which to concentrate for preaching purposes! Here is also a great opportunity for series preaching. Perhaps it should also be added that although the psalm is intended to be a response by the people to the Old Testament lesson, rather than being read as a lesson on its own, that in no way suggests that it cannot be used as the text for the sermon.

A note on language: We have used the term *Old Testament* in this series because that is the language employed by the Consultation on Common Texts. Pastors and worship committees may wish to consider alternative terms, such as *First Testament* or *Hebrew Scriptures,* that do not imply that those writings somehow have less value than the rest of the Christian Bible. Another option is to refer to *First Lesson* (always for the Hebrew Scriptures), *Second Lesson* (from Acts or the epistles), and *Gospel.*

PREACHING AND WORSHIP
AMIDST THE CLASH OF CALENDARS

Perhaps at no other time of the year than in the autumn do preachers and planners of worship experience so many demands upon them for attention by diverse kinds of programmatic and special interest concerns. Three calendars are usually competing for attention all the year round, with varying degrees of success at different times.

The most important, of course, is the Christian year calendar itself, which guides us through the varied acts in the drama of our salvation with commentary provided by the lectionary all along the way. The observance of that calendar and the lectionary keeps the Church faithful to the Easter proclamation, since the purpose of the Christian year is to assist us in examining the Easter mystery from different perspectives. The regular return of the Lord's Day reminds us that we are an Easter people, a product of the eighth day of creation, and that through baptism we have been born from above and are now engaged upon a pilgrimage in which we are seeking the things that are above.

The Church's programmatic calendar is another significant factor in planning for preaching and worship, particularly in the autumn. For many churches this is the time to swing into action after summer recess. Church school resumes, or if it has not stopped, students now move to different classes. Choirs once more reappear, and it is not unknown for "Back to Church Sunday" to be marked by the donning of vestments or robes that were abandoned after Memorial Day. The denomination as well as the local church uses this time to make special emphases. A kind of pan-Protestant calendar observes annually in the autumn Christian Education Sunday, World Communion Sunday, Laity Sunday, Stewardship Sunday, and National Bible Sunday. Depending upon the particular denomination, one may also be expected to observe Reformation Sunday and United Nations Sunday as well. Homecoming Sunday is regularly observed in autumn by many congregations. Frequently these days come equipped by the denominational program agencies with special orders of service, scripture lessons, even sermon outlines. Without denying the legitimacy and appropriateness of the interests represented, it may still be said that among American Protestants the program Sunday threatens to do to the regular pattern of Christian year and lectionary what the saints days did to the dominical pattern of worship in the medieval church.

The civil calendar is the third contender for the attention of the congregation. In some ways the first of September is the beginning of a new year in the civil calendar. The beginning of school might be said to exercise more influence over the national life than any other single event, so by those dates vacations are planned, houses are bought and sold, clothes are purchased, schedules are arranged. Labor Day weekend is a significant date on many counts, and so it is not unusual to find sermon topics for the Sunday that deal not only with labor but with beginnings. Election Day and Veterans Day do not appeal as much to a pulpit setting, but they have been known to become primary themes for the Lord's Day. Perhaps the most difficult issue to deal with in terms of the civil calendar is that of Thanksgiving, because it is so entwined with our national and religious roots. It is easy to forget that Thanksgiving Day is not a day of the Church (eucharistically speaking, for the Church every Sunday is Thanksgiving Day), but is a patriotic occasion dictated by a presidential proclamation. And what the president proclaims is Thanksgiving Day, the fourth Thursday in November, not Thanksgiving Sunday. Yet often a Thanksgiving Sunday is invented so that the people are relieved from the patriotic burden of attending church more than once a week. The Sunday that is thus lost from the Christian year is Christ the King, the very Sunday that allows us to proclaim that we have no time for civil religion and that our citizenship is in heaven!

Because Christianity is incarnational, designed to relate to the world in which we live, all three calendars need to be taken seriously. The question becomes one of deciding how Christian preaching and worship relate to the three and by what principles we set priorities among them. Certain affirmations need to be made and regulations established in order to avoid both liturgical chaos and a homiletical

14

pattern that is only a response to squeaking wheels in church or society. For persons who exercise gospel freedom, law is important because it gives us an excuse for breaking it!

1. We affirm the priority of the Lord's Day as the day of the Christian assembly, which meets primarily for the purpose of retelling the story and responding to the story in sacramental actions.

2. We affirm the priority of the lectionary as the primary means by which the story is told and remembered in an orderly and coherent fashion.

3. We affirm the relevance of the scriptures to Christian living as a gift of God. The Bible is not something we have to "make relevant" to our lives, or through which we search to find relevant passages; as "Word of God" it addresses the depths of our being as we open ourselves to it in earnest prayer and committed study.

4. We affirm the movement from word and sacrament in the assembly to a life of service in the world as the Church becomes God's word and sacrament for the world. Preaching and liturgy lead us to a participation in the sacrificial life of Christ. Christians then have a responsibility to know about the world and its concerns, so that our ministry may be both compassionate and informed.

Adherence to these affirmations can help keep the scriptures at the center of the congregation's worship life without using them in a haphazard fashion to serve some purely thematic end. For example, when confronted with the necessity of preaching on Labor Day weekend, the preacher's pattern should not be to decide what he or she thinks about the labor/management issues of the day and then find some umbrella scripture lesson that might relate in a vague way, but need not be referred to at length. The first Sunday in September will generally have the lessons of Proper Eighteen. The Gospel reading is the story of two healings by Jesus and offers little help. But the Old Testament reading is Proverbs 22, and its affirmation that God is the maker of both rich and poor and that it is God who pleads the cause of the poor. And the epistle lesson is James's concern that our faith be shown by the good works we do relative to the needy. Surely these lessons can lead the preacher to address whatever issues may be significant locally, nationally, or globally for the ordering of the relationships between labor and management or between rich and poor, and the meaning of work in a Christian context.

It must be admitted that the limitations of the lectionary may seem rather obvious for those traditions that celebrate the Eucharist infrequently, but usually on the first Sunday in October, World Communion Sunday. In Year B the preacher is confronted with Satan's challenge to God about Job, the exaltation of Christ in Hebrews, and Jesus' prohibition of divorce and the blessing of the children in Mark! On the face of it, one is inclined to run for cover under other texts. It may be necessary to rid oneself of the impression that the texts (and the sermon) need to deal with the Lord's Supper every time the Lord's Supper is observed. Rather, if the Eucharist is bread for the journey, then it is important to spread the table at the time God's people are confronting head on the tough questions about life and living. The Eucharist is the sign of Christ's continuing, nourishing, supportive presence in the midst of the assembly. When we gather around the dinner table, it is not necessary to discuss the nutritional components of each course for us to benefit from them! In the same way, every aspect of the Lord's Supper need not be cognitively spelled out for individuals and the community to appropriate its power. See the "Celebration" entry for Proper Twenty-two to explore some ways these texts may contribute to a fuller understanding of what it means to discover our unity in the common life God gives around a common table.

The sequential character of the lessons allows for a seasonal series of sermons; only the preacher's imagination can limit how these may be employed. The Old Testament lessons draw from the Wisdom literature and the writings. Four weeks are devoted to Job, providing an opportunity to pose a theodicy for questions of suffering. The stories of Esther, Ruth, and Hannah provide female role models of struggle, faith, and sacrifice. The epistle lessons can allow for an extended series of expository sermons on James and Hebrews. The Gospel lessons are in most cases accounts of Jesus' teaching ministry and lists of his sayings. This may provide an opportunity for a sermon series on the characteristics of the Reign of God, culminating in the Gospel reading from John's Passion narrative on the Festival of Christ

16

the King. Such an arrangement helps illustrate that, for Mark, the ministry of Jesus can only be understood in light of the cross.

As a time of new beginnings, this autumn may also be an opportunity for the preacher to make some New Year's resolutions about preaching. Such resolutions may include fixing a time for study and preparation on one's weekly calendar and keeping to it as inflexibly as one does official board meetings, so that sermon preparation is not relegated to the off-times and the residue of the week. Likewise, disciplined prayer time as preparation for preaching can be worked into the schedule. A daily office should be devised by each working pastor as a means of doing the minimal work of prayer, and it should be adhered to whether one likes it or not, because that is what an office is: *officium,* a duty. There is nothing magical here, but there is something formative for a life in the Spirit that is more than psychological self-help.

The visuals for this long end of the year are green (except for Christ the King and when All Saints is celebrated on the first Sunday in November, and then the color is white or gold). Many churches alter the basic green throughout the autumn to move with the changing color of the leaves, picking up more reds and browns and oranges and yellows. Green should still predominate, however, with its suggestion of life and growth.

Proper Seventeen
Sunday Between August 28
and September 3 Inclusive

Old Testament Texts

Song of Solomon 2:8-13 is a love poem. Psalm 45 is a royal psalm that celebrates the marriage of the king.

The Lesson: *Song of Solomon 2:8-13*

A Springtime Love Poem

Setting. The title of this book in the NRSV is The Song of Solomon. The opening verse, however, provides another name, The Song of Songs. Although the book is referred to with both names, the latter name is probably more insightful. The syntactical construction, Song of Songs, is the way to state the superlative in Hebrew. Thus the book could also be entitled, The Greatest Song. The Greatest Song consists of the celebration of love. The twenty-five to thirty separate love poems that have been collected in the book celebrate all aspects of love, from tentative courtship with all the fantasies of love that accompany initial attraction to secret encounters with the joy of physical sexuality. Because of its character as an anthology, the book is difficult to date. Some speculate that the poems may go back as far as the early Solomonic period—hence it is attributed to Solomon. More clear is the collecting and editing of this poetry in a post-exilic setting.

Structure. Most scholars agree that the Song of Songs is made up of disparate poems that functioned independently. There is debate, however, whether the poems are presently meant to be read independently, or whether they now function as a larger drama. Clearly there are changes of voice throughout the poetry. There are the female and male lovers, who exchange love poems, and, perhaps, a chorus of voices that provides reflection and commentary. Whether these voices present a larger story is a debate that cannot be settled here. Nevertheless, it is important to listen for the different voices in the poetry, for at least two are present in Song of Songs 2:8-13: the female lover in vv. 8-10 and the male lover in vv. 11-13.

Significance. Song of Songs 2:8-13 describes a springtime courtship. It begins with the female lover who hears her beloved from a distance, looks out and watches him approach. The imagery is sexual. He is like a young stag. He peeks into her house and then speaks in vv. 10-13. "It is spring," he tells his lover. "Winter is past, flowers are out, trees are budding, and their fragrance fills the air. Come away with me!" The lectionary breaks off at this point, but the text probably doesn't. It should include at least v. 14, where the male lover continues his speech. He wishes to enjoy all the little physical aspects of his beloved—her face, her voice—while the two of them are hidden away someplace in the privacy of the rocky clefts.

Traditionally the Song of Songs has been read on two levels: as secular love poetry and as theological metaphor of God and the people of God or Jesus and the Church. Often the two levels of reading are interpreted as an either/or dichotomy in which the reader picks and chooses how to read the material. As secular love poetry the sensual and sexual nature of the material is emphasized. As theological metaphor a more sanitized relationship between Jesus and the Church is explored. Such a dichotomy hinders interpretation for at least two reasons. First, there was no such thing as secular love poetry in ancient Israel, at least as we would conceive of it today. God and sexuality were a frequent combination in the ancient Near East, with the result that the act of sex, itself, became a sacrament at the heart of worship. Thus, a sexual relationship with God was not a metaphor but a fact for Israel. Cult prostitution is a common motif in prophetic condemnation of Israel's worship (see Hosea), not because it was pornographic (that is, a secular misuse of sexuality), but because it was idolatrous (that is, a sacred misuse of sexuality). Love poetry, therefore, was never simply secular for Israel. The divine always loomed in the background. Second, when the dichotomy between a literal, secular reading of Song of Songs and a metaphorical, sacred reading is neatly separated at the outset, then the metaphorical reading loses its power and is instead reduced to the well-worn analogy that Jesus is the bridegroom and the Church is the bride. Such a reading is certainly appropriate, but the power of the metaphorical language requires that it be read first as love poetry, with all the passion and physical quality that falling in love demands. Only with the power of real sexual drive in the background does the overwhelming force of the metaphor of falling in love with God come into focus.

The Song of Songs provides an excellent example of the twists and turns that cultures go through and the problems of historical hermeneutics that arise because of it. The problem with the Song of Songs for ancient Israel is that there was not a dichotomy between the literal and the metaphorical. Scholars speculate that this may be the reason why it took the book so long to enter the Canon. Our problem is that tradition has succeeded too well in separating the literal and the metaphorical, and we have lost the raw passion of the text, with its celebration of sexuality. A quote from Rabbi Akiva—who fought to include the Song of Songs in the Canon, against the wishes of his colleagues who wanted to ban the text—provides a fitting conclusion to our commentary. He states, ''The entire universe is not as worthy as the day on which the Song of Songs was given to Israel, for all the Writings are holy, but the Song of Songs is the Holy of Holies'' (*Mishnah Yadayim* 3:5). Such a conclusion requires that one understand the power of the subject matter of the text.

The Response: *Psalm 45:1-2, 6-9*

A Royal Marriage

Setting. There is debate over the setting of this psalm. It is unparalleled in the psalter. Clearly it is celebrating a marriage of the monarch, but what is the occasion? Is it a historical marriage or is it a sacral marriage? The reference to the daughter of Tyre in v. 12 suggests a specific, historical event. Yet the clear cultic setting has raised the suspicion that Psalm 45 may be part of an annual ritual. The important point for using the psalm on this Sunday is certainly the link between the love poetry in the Song of Songs and the marriage festival in Psalm 45.

Structure. The lectionary reading is somewhat choppy. It includes the opening two verses (vv. 1-2) and vv. 6-9. The larger psalm might be separated into two parts. Verses 1-8 describe the king and the power of his anointing, while vv. 9-17 describe the marriage of the king and queen. The lectionary reading includes the opening and closing verses of the first section of the psalm (vv. 1-2, 6-8) and the opening verse of the marriage (v. 9). Absent from the lectionary text is the warrior imagery used to describe the king in vv. 3-5, the address to the queen in vv. 10-15, and the prophetic speech to the king, which concludes the psalm in vv. 16-17.

Significance. Two motifs stand out in the psalm: The anointing of the king and the marriage. The anointing of the king dominates in the lectionary reading. The speaker is identified in v. 1, and the king is addressed in v. 2. The language describing the king is superlative. He is the most beautiful human in the world; therefore God blessed him (v. 3). The power of this blessing is described through the warrior imagery in vv. 3-5, before the lectionary text picks up again in v. 6. Here a problem of interpretation arises. The NRSV translates, "Your throne, O God, endures forever and ever." Upon first reading this appears to be a reference to God, but the entire hymn is focused on the king, which suggests that the king being referred to here is God. Thus is the superlative language a reference to the king or is the statement an address to God? A clear answer is not possible, but the focus is certainly on the king once again in vv. 7b-8 where the anointing of the monarch is described. The anointing of the king functions as preparation for marriage, which is only hinted at in the lectionary text in v. 9.

New Testament Texts

Our lessons begin a new series of sequential readings from the Epistle of James and the gospel according to Mark. The readings from James, which extend across five weeks, are the only occurrence of this letter in the three years of the lectionary cycle. At this point, however, we are simply returning to Mark, which is the major Gospel for

Year B. In a remarkable way, both texts for this week address the question of what makes religion genuine.

The Epistle: *James 1:17-27*

The Positive and Negative Sides of Pure Religion

Setting. The entire Epistle of James is parenesis. Only v. 1 of chapter 1 resembles a Greco-Roman letter in form. Otherwise this so-called letter most resembles ancient Stoic moral philosophy and Jewish moral exhortation—and far more the latter than the former. Scholars debate the identity of the author, James. Some defend the traditional identification of this James as the brother of the Lord who was a key leader in the Jerusalem church, but most conclude because of the highly literate Greek in which the document is written and the apparent awareness of Paul's teachings that the author is actually unknown except as "James."

In general, chapter 1 of James is a loose assemblage of originally independent sayings. After the epistolary opening (1:1), James calls the readers to be steadfast when tempted. He argues that as they are tested, their faith produces endurance that leads to perfection. This manner of life is contrasted with foolish living, which runs from desire to sin to death.

Structure. Those who study this letter diligently find that it lacks a carefully defined structure. Within the heart of the letter (2:1–3:12) there are clearly identifiable units of material in which one is able to follow the pattern of the author's thought, and in other parts of the letter the passages seem related by catchwords. But in many instances there is no discernible reason for a series of passages to be set in their current order.

After establishing the framework of the letter's basic concerns in 1:2-16, the author moves in 1:17-27 to tell the reader four things he wants to be sure they know, so that they will not be deceived (v. 16). James writes of (1) the origin of what is good (vv. 17-18); (2) the style of a righteous life (vv. 19-21); (3) the necessity of active devotion (vv. 22-25); and (4) the qualities of "pure" religion (vv. 26-27). The matters are related in a pattern of evolving thought.

Significance. Throughout this letter James advocates a rigorous, disciplined moral existence. The author makes clear distinctions between right and wrong, and he is persuaded and seeks to persuade his readers that believers are to live righteously. James teaches that believers are engaged in a struggle between desiring to sin and desiring to do what is right. Nevertheless, James is not the kind of thinker who contends that believers pull themselves up by their bootstraps. "Every perfect gift," says James, came down from "the Father of lights." It is "the implanted word that has the power to save [believers'] souls" (v. 21). Yet James mightily exhorts his readers to "welcome with meekness" this saving word. James is convinced that as the word comes to the believers, and the believers open themselves to the presence and power of this word in their lives, they will be able to defeat the desire to sin that is within them, because God's word is powerful unto salvation.

All James says should be viewed in relation to this particular outlook. Thus, when James calls to the readers to listen, to be slow to speak, and to be slow to anger, he is not merely saying "be good." He is concerned with righteousness, not mere niceness. The tendency to hasty, angry talk thwarts the ability to hear the saving word of God. The problem James addresses is not simple rudeness, but rather it is a style of life that excludes God's will because one yields readily to the desire to sin. Believers must deliberately make a place in their lives for the hearing of God's saving word.

James continues, calling the readers beyond sheer listening. Merely listening to God's word is itself not the accomplishment of righteousness. One listens to resist the desire to sin, but a passive life of not sinning is not the reality of righteousness. True hearing generates an active life of faith, and it is such a life that James is concerned for the readers to live. "Be doers of the word, and not merely hearers who deceive themselves," says James. And here, he puts his finger on a rotten form of piety that hoodwinks believers into thinking that they are Christian because of what they do not do. James argues there are things believers should not do, but he also argues that simply not doing such things is not a true life of faith.

Thus James calls the readers to action, giving them complementary illustrations of pure religion. Real religion puts checks on our lives and generates active compassion toward those in need. Resisting evil and doing good is pure religion.

The Gospel: *Mark 7:1-8, 14-15, 21-23*

Whose Values Are Your Values?

Setting. We last worked with Mark as the Gospel reading for Proper Eleven. We treated the final sections of Mark 6 at that time. Our lesson today resumes the sequential readings from Mark by taking up the next section of the Gospel. The entirety of 7:1-23 is devoted to the theme of the tradition of the elders. Our lesson is an abbreviated form of the passage, which aims at coherence and concision but which may prove distracting for reading in worship; for more than one hearer (not to mention those following the lesson in their own Bibles) will wonder why two sets of verses were skipped. Sadly, such healthy curiosity may prevent careful consideration of the text; and so, perhaps one should read all of 7:1-23 and, then, simply deal with the coherent materials identified by the lectionary reading. But, even if the abridged version of the text is read, notice that the point of Jesus' critique of the Pharisees is most clearly stated in v. 8, which should be read with vv. 1-7.

Structure. The three pieces from 7:1-23 are parts of the two basic sections of this text, 7:1-13 and 7:14-27. The first of these sections declares the inappropriateness of substituting human religious practices (ritual) in the place of active concern with God's will (compassion); the second section proclaims that the true condition of one's life is known by the products of one's living, not merely by the superficial rituals one performs.

Significance. The basic story told in this lesson is a controversy. Jesus is criticized for the laxness of his disciples' religious practices, and he bluntly critiques the superfluous character of some so-called religion. The tone of the narrative is polemical, probably reflecting the energy of both Jesus' debates with the Pharisees and the later Church's struggles with the Judaism out of which it came. While the basic points of the two major sections of 7:1-23 are essentially negative, there are positive declarations and implications in the passage that will inspire preaching other than against something.

Before considering the lessons of this lesson, we need to recognize the distance between our world and the one in which this story was told. For the citizens of the first-century Mediterranean world, especially its eastern regions, the matters of "clean and unclean" were fundamental religious categories. Through the issue of purity ancients addressed their concern for distinguishing the sacred and the profane. The world was structured through purity codes so that people, things, times, and places could be evaluated as godly or ungodly. Above all, God was pure and concerned with purity. We are heirs to this thinking when we mouth lines such as, "Cleanliness is next to godliness"—something we still say but probably do not really believe. At best we translate, "It's better to smell good than to stink." When Jesus and the early Christians criticized the religious preoccupation with purity codes, they were in essence—and the other ancients got the point—criticizing a concept of God. The stakes in ancient debates about "clean and unclean" were very high. People lived and died by the practice of purity codes because they believed that these regulations had everything to do with God.

Jesus called the God and the religion of purity codes into question, and like the prophets of old he called people beyond mere ritual to genuine devotion to living out God's will. If the crud that comes out of a human life reflects the corruption of that person's soul, then the good that comes forth in the course of living demonstrates the health and wholeness of one's life. If this is the case, and we appraise the matter theologically, then God is concerned that our inner dispositions and our actual lives be congruent in terms of active good. In turn, if this is true, then God is not removed from life into a heavenly compartment of super-purity; rather God is present and active in the world, especially in the hearts and lives of truly religious people, accomplishing that which is good, honest, compassionate, generous, and of lasting value. God's glory is grace, not sanitation.

The words of Jesus are both liberating and irritating. He refuses to allow us the comfort of a carefully prescribed and regulated religion. There is no easy parade for the kind of piety Jesus talks about. It should not surprise us that the Jesus who spoke in this manner died on a cross. What carefully constructed religious system could ever evaluate the purity of that cross?

Proper 17: The Celebration

The preacher who wonders what to do with today's lesson from the Song of Solomon may be amazed to learn that St. Bernard preached eighty-six sermons on the book and never got beyond the beginning of the third chapter! That was, of course, the twelfth century and very different theories of homiletics and hermeneutics prevailed, but the sermons may still be read with profit as an exercise in dialogue between scriptural images. A particularly beautiful example is his commentary on the passage in today's lesson, "the voice of the turtledove is heard in our land."

> Can this statement, so unusual, or even, if I may say it, so unworthy of God, lack significance? Nowhere, I think, will you find him speaking like this of heaven, nowhere else like this of earth. Notice then the utter happiness of hearing the God of heaven say: "in our land." . . . This is clearly not the language of domination but of fellowship and intimate friendship. He speaks as Bridegroom, not as lord. Think of it! He is the Creator, and he makes himself one of us? It is love that speaks, that knows no lordship. This is a song of love, in fact, and meant to be sustained only by lovers, not by others. God loves too, though not through a gift distinct from himself: he is himself the source of all loving. And therefore it is all the more vehement, for he does not possess love, he is love. And those whom he loves he calls friends, not servants. The master has become the friend, for he would not have called the disciples friends if it were not true. (Bernard of Clairvaux, *On the Song of Songs III*, trans. Kilian Walsh and Irene Edmonds, Cistercian Fathers Series, no. 31 [Kalamazoo, Mich.: Cistercian Publications, 1979], pp. 120-21)

Charles Wesley, never daunted by any passage of scripture, also penned lines based on verses from today's Old Testament lesson. They may be sung to St. Catherine and serve as a response to the lesson. Because Wesley interprets the reference to winter as death and the "arise" as the summons to resurrection, the hymn may need some explanation, or the second stanza may be used by itself.

> Jesus, as taught by thee, I pray,
> preserve me till I see thy light;
> still let me for thy coming stay,
> stop a poor wavering sinner's flight;
> till thou my full Redeemer art
> O keep, in mercy keep my heart.

O might I hear the turtle's voice,
the cooing of thy gentle dove,
the call that bids my heart rejoice:
"Arise, and come away, my love!
The storm is gone, the winter's o'er;
arise, for thou shalt weep no more!"

Give me to bow with thee my head,
and sink into the silent grave,
to rest among the quiet dead
till thou display thy power to save,
thy resurrection's power exert,
and rise triumphant in my heart!

The following stanza was printed by John Wesley in the 1780 Collection as the first stanza to the hymn we now know as "Christ, Whose Glory Fills the Skies." Its first and last lines are based on Song of Solomon 2:14, 13 respectively. It may be used by itself as a sung introit or call to worship or used with its original stanzas as one of the hymns for the service.

O disclose thy lovely face!
Quicken all my drooping powers!
Gasps my fainting soul for grace
as a thirsty land for showers:
haste, my Lord, no more delay!
Come, my Savior, come away!

Today's Epistle lesson directs us to the first stanza of "Great Is Thy Faithfulness" (AMEC *Bicentennial Hymnal*, no. 84; *The Baptist Hymnal*, 1991, no. 54; *Hymns for the Family of God*, no. 98; *The Presbyterian Hymnal*, 1990, no. 276; *United Methodist Hymnal*, no. 140).

Proper Eighteen
Sunday Between September
4 and 10 Inclusive

Old Testament Texts

Proverbs 22:1-2, 8-9, 22-23 explores godly conduct especially in dealing with the poor. Psalm 125 is a song of trust that employs wisdom language.

The Lesson: *Proverbs 22:1-2, 8-9, 22-23*

Acting with Integrity

Setting. Wisdom literature arises out of the theological insight that God permeates all of life, and that because of this, there are set structures in the creation that humans must recognize and then live by. Wisdom is a two-part process in which the sage first seeks to recognize the divine order in creation and, second, attempts to live in harmony with it. Wisdom, therefore, is both intellectual and practical because ultimately it is theological. By uncovering the fundamental order to the cosmos and then acting in harmony with it, the wise person is brought closer to God. Thus, good moral conduct strengthens not only humans but the whole fabric of creation, while, conversely, bad conduct (action out of harmony with God's created order) weakens humanity and the creation itself.

Proverbs (Hebrew, *mašal*) are one way in which the sages sought to communicate divine wisdom. An essential component to the proverb is an analogy that is based on experience. Wisdom teachers sought to teach the often unseen and unknown structures of creation to others by comparing an experienced truth with an outcome that might not be experienced by all. In other words, by comparing at the level of shared past experience, the sages sought to construct a body of fundamental truths about God and creation that might in fact shape future experience. The Hebrew word for proverb (*mašal*) carries this two-part meaning. It signifies both analogy based on experience and the power of a word to rule (that is to shape experience). Cervantes put it this way: "A proverb is a short sentence founded upon long experience containing a truth." We might restate Cervantes' conclusion with the following technical language: A proverb is a similitude that is meant to function paradigmatically through time.

Structure. There is a loose structure to the book of Proverbs that could be separated into nine parts: (1) chapters 1–9, (2) 10:1–22:16, (3) 22:17–24:22, (4) 24:23-34, (5) 25–29, (6) 30:1-9, (7) 30:10-33, (8) 31:1-9, (9) 31:10-31. For the purpose of interpreting the present lectionary text, it is noteworthy that Proverbs 22:1-2, 8-9, 22-23 is a collection of texts from two different sections in the book. Proverbs 22:1-2, 8-9 are part of a section that begins with the heading "the proverbs of Solomon" in 10:1 and continues through 22:16. This section is made up of single-sentence proverbs that render detached, impersonal generalizations about life. Proverbs 22:22-23 is included in the section 22:17–24:34, which is labeled "the words of the wise." Here the style changes from the impersonal generalizations of the sayings to more direct imperatives, where specific commands and prohibitions are set forth.

Significance. Content is what links the different texts together. The topic of rich and poor is touched upon from a number of different perspectives, but the one being addressed throughout is the rich or powerful person.

Proverbs 22:1-2. Verse 1 provides a framework or perspective in which wealth must be evaluated. The text is not a polemic against wealth per se. Rather it is meant to place wealth within a larger context, and, in so doing, it critically evaluates those who would give it highest priority. The central point of the text is that reputation (literally "a name" in Hebrew) and personal qualities (literally "charm" or "grace" in Hebrew) are the fundamental values for evaluating persons, rather than their status from wealth. Verse 2 would seem to build on the conclusion of v. 1 by leveling any distinction between humans on the basis of wealth, with the affirmation that all humans are created by God.

Proverbs 22:8-9 includes two proverbs. Verse 8 explores the inevitable consequences of evil actions. It begins by describing evil within the limits of controlled human action, "whoever sows injustice." The Hebrew word for injustice is *'awlah,* meaning wickedness or actions to which God is not connected. The second part of the proverb, "will reap calamity," describes the result of such human action with language that hints at larger consequences. The Hebrew word for calamity is *'awen,* meaning "uncanny or magical power," which takes on connotations of weird or supernatural forces. The last line of v. 8 is meant to describe the end result of destruction that awaits such a person. The Hebrew, unfortunately, is unclear. The NRSV translation, "and the rod of anger will fail" has been amended by commentators to read, "the rod of his excess smites him," which, although it is a conjecture, makes better sense. Verse 9 reintroduces the motif of the poor, in order to make the following paradoxical statement. The person with a "good eye" (NRSV, "those who are generous") is blessed, because that person gives bread to the poor. In other words, the one who does not live for self, achieves self-fulfillment (is blessed).

Proverbs 22:22-23. The generalized statements about life give way to direct command in vv. 22-23. The language in this more extended saying presupposes a legal context. The point is that the more powerful must not use the legal system to their advantage against the less powerful simply because they have more money or power to manipulate the system. Verse 22 gives the imperative: Do not rob (literally "wrest away the right of" in Hebrew) the poor simply because they are poor. Do not crush the afflicted at the gate (the equivalent of the law court in ancient Israel). In other words, the command is that the powerful not use the legitimate structures of law as a form of oppression, simply because they can afford to do so and it is technically legal. Verse 23 provides the theological reasons for the prohibition. (1) Yahweh will take up the brief and defend the case of the oppressed one. (2) And, afterward, Yahweh will switch roles and become the prosecutor, who will seek the death penalty for the oppressor. The proverb is a condemnation of a litigious society.

This sequence of proverbs requires three focuses in preaching. The first issue that the preacher must address is whether we actually believe the fundamental starting point of the sages, that God permeates all of life, and that, because of this, there are set structures in creation that must be followed. The second issue is the development of theme that arises from the combination of the lectionary text. Does our belief in a divine morality within creation ever require that we not pursue our own self-interest even when it is perfectly legal? And, third, then what does it mean to be human and what is self-fulfillment for Christians?

The Response: *Psalm 125*

Trusting God

Setting. Psalm 125 is a song of trust in a situation of oppression. Note how in v. 3 the singer is not in a situation of having power but under the rule of another. The language suggests that Israel was under foreign rule whenever this psalm was written. The psalm, therefore, is not presenting an idyllic picture of trusting in God. In fact, much of the language is complaint in vv. 4-5.

Structure. Psalm 125 moves through three parts. It begins with words of trust in vv. 1-2, provides the reason why trust is needed in describing how the land is under foreign rule in v. 3, and then concludes with petition and complaint in vv. 4-5.

Significance. Psalm 125 illustrates the fundamental belief of the wisdom school that was described above. Yet it explores this belief in just the opposite context—of oppression rather than from the vantage point of being secure in power. It is a confession of trust in God in a time when life circumstances would lead to another conclusion. The opening language differs from that of the sages in that the imagery of Zion is used to describe the secure foundations of the created order, rather than proverbs. The point, however, is the same. Certain fundamental beliefs about God and creation must inform the action of the people of God in all circumstances—when they are in power and can manipulate legal systems in their favor (so Proverbs 22:22-23), or when they are on the other end of the spectrum and experience oppression from others (Psalm 125). Trust in God is the constant factor between these two poles, which must inform all moral behavior.

New Testament Texts

The lessons from James and Mark continue. In both cases we merely move ahead to the next unit of material as the authors lead us. The topics, however, change dramatically from last week's lessons.

The Epistle: *James 2:1-10 (11-13), 14-17*

The Problem of Partiality and the Case for Good Works

Setting. For general remarks about James refer to last week's lessons.

Our lesson comes from the central section of the epistle, 2:1–3:12. There we find a series of three discourses on themes of crucial concern to James. James 2:1-13 is a bold warning against partiality; 2:14-26 takes up the well-known theme of "faith versus works"; and 3:1-12 treats the topic of "the tongue" in a set of ways.

Structure. Those who diligently study this letter find that it lacks a carefully defined structure. Yet, in the heart of the letter there are clearly identifiable units of material in which one is able to follow the pattern of the author's thought, and in other parts of the letter the passages seem related by catchwords. The verses of our lesson come from two of the more clearly defined portions of the letter. The combination in the lectionary is a bit curious. There is a loose connection between the section on partiality (2:1-13) and the following treatment of "faith and works" (2:14-26) in that believers are not to be partial against the poor, and faith and works orient the good actions of believers toward the needy. But, either section could stand alone as well as in the combination suggested here.

Significance. In the first chapter James called his fellow believers to a life of faith, perseverance, and perfection and away from a life of desire, sin, and death. In the opening discourse of the central section of the letter he vividly illustrates the corrupt results of choosing the wrong way of life. The way of desire and sin leads, in this world, to a form of community life in which those who enjoy and display the benefits of material wealth are given favorable treatment, while those who are this world's "have-nots" are disregarded, discounted, and even disgraced. First, James states that such behavior runs contrary to the revealed will of God known in God's own choice of the poor to be rich in faith. Then, he illustrates the stupidity of such partiality in the Christian community by referring to the incongruity between favored treatment of the rich and the rotten treatment of the Christian community by the rich themselves. Finally, James judges the invalidity of this form of life in Christian community by declaring that such favoritism is a breach of the law "You shall love your neighbor as yourself." This declaration comes from Leviticus 19:18, and James calls it "the royal law" perhaps because of the frequent memory in the gospel tradition of Jesus' promulgation of this particular teaching (see, e.g., Mark 12:31). It is cast here as the hallmark of Christian life.

The optional verses (vv. 11-13) are difficult. Briefly, James is employing an argument typical of Jewish defenses of the law as a unity. One cannot pick and choose at will among the commandments. James seems to contend that God's whole law is valid for humanity, and as a gift from God it directs life into the path of righteousness. This high valuing of the law is typical of a segment of the earliest Church, and in the context of the New Testament we see that among the earliest believers there were different sensibilities about the place and role of the law in Christian life.

Verses 14-17 come from the second discourse in the center of the letter. Here we find the basis of the old "Paul versus James" debate about "faith versus works." Frankly James's juxtaposition of faith to works and his use of terminology ("have faith but do not have works") are awkward. This does not appear to be James's own mode of thinking. His references to "someone" who speaks of "faith apart from works" indicates that he is replying to something he has heard but does not believe or even fully comprehend. James allows that we can distinguish faith and works, but in Christian life they are not alternatives. Faith issues in works, and works indicate faith. James declares that "a person is justified by works and not by faith alone."

Remarkably Paul never says that one is justified by faith alone, for such an intellectual notion of faith would make no sense to him. For Paul faith means that believers walk in the Spirit in love, which is probably what James means by "good works." James's awkward argument is nothing more than a theological version of the maxim, "Actions speak louder than words."

The Gospel: *Mark 7:24-37*

Grace Overtaking Boundaries

Setting. Leaving the debates between Jesus and the Pharisees behind, we move with Mark to consider Jesus' interactions with a Gentile woman whose child was ill and with a man who could not hear and had a speech impediment. These are two distinct texts, and one is wise to treat them accordingly. The revised lectionary adds the story of the woman because, like the story of the man who could not hear, the parallel story in Matthew is not included in the lectionary. (See Matthew 15:21-31.) Still it will probably prove impossible to treat both texts, but with planning the one not chosen may be treated in three years! We shall consider the stories together and, then, separately.

Structure. There are two clear stories, that of Jesus and the woman in vv. 24-30 and that of Jesus and the man in vv. 31-37. Apart from Jesus' peculiar acts in taking the man aside privately and, then, in telling those who knew of the healing to tell no one, this is a typical ancient miracle story with problem, action for solution, and confirmation. These elements are present also in the story of Jesus' healing of the woman's daughter, but the spirited conversation between Jesus and the woman actually takes over the narrative.

Significance. These stories are part of a second cycle of miracle accounts that come in Mark's story of Jesus' ministry. One point that makes these healings comparable is that both the woman and the man were outcasts in polite first-century Jewish society. Both were doubly unacceptable—one as a Gentile and a woman, and the other as hearing impaired and speech impaired. These stories make sense in the wake of the debates about "clean and unclean" things in the preceding portion of Mark 7, because for different reasons (Gentile and disabled) these people were regarded as unclean. That the woman was a woman made little or no difference here, since her ethnic origin completely obscured her femaleness for Jewish religious purposes. Had she married a Jew and become a Jewish proselyte, then, her gender would have given her a lesser status—but that issue is unrelated to the dynamics of this text. As a final general observation, Jesus himself has more difficulty seeing God's grace extended across ethnic boundaries than across the lines of physical ability and disability, although in both cases he "comes through."

The story of Jesus and the woman is one of those accounts that has a high claim to authenticity because it is awkward—that is, Jesus does not appear here in the best light! This is not the kind of story that later Christians seeking to enhance the image of Jesus would be likely to embellish. Jesus understands that his mission is to Israel. While it is true that he implies that later there may be a time for ministry among the Gentiles, still his statement shows a limited perspective, and his initial refusal seems insulting. Commentators like to say that Jesus' word for "dogs" is a term for cute little puppies or house pets, but so what! Puppy dogs are not humans and the contrast with "the children" suggests second-class citizenship at best.

The woman's statement, however, which wins Jesus' favor, is an indication of her faith in him. She sees God's power in Jesus, and she believes that God's grace is sufficient for all in need. There is no exhausting God's grace. The woman says this and Jesus knows it. Strange that this realization did not occur to Jesus, but we should take comfort that even our Lord was in need of learning and sometimes got it. The story recognizes the genuine humanity of Jesus, but it also indicates the coherence of his life with the nature of divine grace. God's grace knows no boundaries, but in our world they exist all the same. Yet, God's grace is boundless, and in Jesus Christ even the seemingly insurmountable barriers are crossed.

The healing of the man with hearing and speech problems is told graphically. With the striking line, "his tongue was released," Mark gives us a crucial interpretive pointer. Jesus' ministry is one of liberation. Jesus works to set us free from the real restrictions that reduce our lives to a level less than God's intention. Jesus comes for freedom and wholeness. Indeed in v. 32 Mark may offer us further help. The term for "had an impediment in his speech" is a single, very unusual Greek word. It occurs in the Greek version of Isaiah 35:6, part of the poetic description of God's acts of salvation on the day of final judgment. In healing this man, Jesus sets him free, thus doing the work of God as God's agent of eschatological salvation or ultimate saving grace.

Proper 18: The Celebration

Today's lessons, with their emphasis on the care of the poor and God's gracious reaching out to the needy through Christ, complement the celebration of the Lord's Supper and the observance of Labor Day. This can be a time to rediscover the importance of the offertory as a part of the eucharistic action. In the early church, gifts of bread and wine and other items such as fruit, cheese, oil, and olives were brought by the people and presented at the offertory. The priest took as much as was needed for the eucharistic offering and after the service the deacons distributed the remainder of the gifts to the needy in the community. In other words, it was not possible to come to communion without at the same time caring for the less fortunate. The gifts brought were a sign of God's gifts given to humankind and produced through human labor. In the Christian community, then, one's labor was not for oneself alone. This new offertory prayer in the Roman Missal, based on Jewish forms, has become widely popular in other denominations as well because it recognizes the place of labor in the eucharistic gifts, which we offer as physical food and drink and then receive back as spiritual nourishment.

Blessed are you, Lord, God of all creation:
through your goodness we have this bread to offer,
which earth has given and human hands have made;
it will become for us the bread of life.
Blessed be God for ever.

Blessed are you, Lord, God of all creation:
through your goodness we have this wine to offer,
fruit of the vine and work of human hands;
it will become our spiritual drink.
Blessed be God for ever.

An appropriate offertory hymn, because of its concluding lines, "Be thou for us in life our daily bread," is "God of Our Life, Through

All the Circling Years'' (*The Book of Hymns*, United Methodist, 1964, no. 47; *Hymns for the Living Church*, no. 326; *The Mennonite Hymnal*, 1969, no. 603; *The Presbyterian Hymnal*, 1990, no. 275).

Today's Gospel lesson is the source for the ''gather up the crumbs under thy table'' image in Cranmer's ''Prayer of Humble Access.'' Although that prayer has been omitted from many revised liturgies, it would not be inappropriate as a prayer of preparation printed for private use at the beginning of the bulletin or as a unison conclusion to the Prayers of the People. Following are two versions as it is now employed in the Church of England. The first is a light revision of the traditional form in the Book of Common Prayer (1662), and the second is a new work by Professor David L. Frost.

We do not presume
to come to this your table, merciful Lord,
trusting in our own righteousness,
but in your manifold and great mercies.
We are not worthy
so much as to gather up the crumbs under your table.
But you are the same Lord
whose nature is always to have mercy.
Grant us therefore, gracious Lord,
so to eat the flesh of your dear son Jesus Christ
and to drink his blood,
that we may evermore dwell in him
and he in us. Amen.

Most merciful Lord,
your love compels us to come in.
Our hands were unclean,
our hearts were unprepared;
we were not fit
even to eat the crumbs from under your table.
But you, Lord, are the God of our salvation,
and share your bread with sinners.
So cleanse and feed us
with the precious body and blood of your Son,
that he may live in us and we in him;
and that we, with the whole company of Christ,
may sit and eat in your kingdom. Amen.

Proper Nineteen
Sunday Between September
11 and 17 Inclusive

Old Testament Texts

Proverbs 1:20-33 is a speech by Wisdom. Psalm 19 is a hymn to creation and a celebration of Torah.

The Lesson: *Proverbs 1:20-33*

The Voice of Wisdom

Setting. Wisdom is personified in the Old Testament lesson as a woman. This personification takes place at least three times in Proverbs 1–9. In Proverbs 1:20-33 the woman, Wisdom, calls in the marketplace and admonishes those who pass by to pay attention to her. She reappears in Proverbs 8, where she once again admonishes those who pass by (vv. 1-21), before recounting her special role in creation as the first work of God and his daily delight (vv. 22-31). Finally Wisdom appears one last time in Proverbs 9:1-6, where she invites those who seek after her to enter her house and to feast with her. This personification alerts us to the vital role of wisdom in Israelite life. Wisdom is not simply a storehouse of knowledge that leads to a set body of law, by which life can be managed. Wisdom is alive—a woman with her own emotions and sexuality. She can admonish in the marketplace and seduce persons into her house. Giving in to the seduction of Wisdom is life that leads to the fear of God.

Structure. Proverbs 1:20-33 separates into five parts. Verses 20-21 establish the setting of Wisdom in the marketplace. Note how Wisdom is not the speaker here, but, instead, is referred to in the third person ("Wisdom cries . . . "; "She cries out . . . "). The speech of wisdom begins with a question in vv. 22-23, which sets the mood of the speech. The audience in the marketplace are the simple ones—namely, those who are not heeding the voice of Wisdom. Thus they are fools who hate knowledge, and the speech that follows is one of admonition and disgust.

The results of this situation are sketched out in two speeches in vv. 24-28 and 29-31. Note how each of these speeches begins with the word *because*. The message of the first (vv. 24-28) is that because the call of Wisdom was ignored when the inevitable tragic results of this are played out, Wisdom will laugh at the calamity and not heed any last-minute requests for quick-fix solutions. The message of the second speech (vv. 29-31) is essentially the same as the first, yet it is noteworthy that the theological grounds for rejecting Wisdom are laid out more clearly—to reject Wisdom is to deny any fear of God. The section ends in vv. 32-33 with a concluding contrast. It is important to see that the contrast here is not between the simpleminded and the smart, but between the simpleminded and the listener.

Significance. As the remarks in the previous paragraph indicate, Proverbs 1:20-33 should be read with an eye on the larger context of Proverbs 1–9, where Wisdom is personified in a number of places (Proverbs 1, 8, 9). What does this mean, and how should we preach this material?

First, and foremost, the personification of Wisdom suggests a high degree of theological reflection concerning her authority as either an independent or dependent attribute of God. Proverbs 1:20-33 presupposes this authority without exploring the relationship between God and Wisdom in any specific detail. Verse 29 simply states that to reject Wisdom is the same as not fearing God. This relationship is explored in more detail in Proverbs 8:22, and the reader is encouraged to read the commentaries on what it means that Wisdom was "created" at the "beginning" and thus is the "first" of God's acts of long ago.

Second, the authority of Wisdom is important for interpreting her frustration in the marketplace in 1:20-33. Notice that there is really no teaching or persuasion in this text, which one expects from the

Wisdom tradition. Rather the discourse of Wisdom is more reminiscent of prophetic speech. As is frequent in the prophets, the discourse is taking place in the center of everyone's activity in the marketplace. There is reproof, threat of punishment, and direct claims of authority without evidence from experience. See, for example, Isaiah 65:12b, where the prophet sounds very much like Wisdom in the marketplace:

> because, when I called, you did not answer,
> when I spoke, you did not listen,
> but you did what was evil in my sight,
> and chose what I did not delight in.

Third, it is clear from this text that Wisdom is competing for the attention of the people, and is disgusted with the marginal role that she is allotted. Her competition is also personified as either a Foolish Woman (9:1-6) or as an Adulterous Woman (Proverbs 5, 6, 7). Although most interpreters emphasize merely the social aspect of the teaching against the adulteress, certainly, she must also be personified on a larger social and religious level over against Wisdom. When viewed in this way it becomes clear that life is filled with seduction. All persons in the marketplace are being seduced by competing female powers in Proverbs 1–9. Each woman has her own house and seeks to draw persons inside. The difference is that one is the way of insight and life, while the other is death (Wisdom, 9:1-6; Folly, 9:13-18). This final contrast is the point of departure for preaching Proverbs 1:20-33, but the contrast must be brought into the present time—perhaps as a contrast between certain social values (Folly) and the Church (Wisdom). Think about your church and your social context. What are the seductions that most influence your situation? Personify them into Folly or an Adulteress and interpret the admonition of Wisdom in 1:20-33 over against them.

The Response: *Psalm 19*

In Praise of Torah

Setting. Psalm 19 perhaps consists of two separate psalms. Verses 1-6 are a hymn to creation and vv. 7-14 are a meditation on Torah, employing wisdom language.

Structure. The hymn to creation has two parts: the silent voice of creation (vv. 1-4), and the sun (vv. 5-6). The power of creation to bring forth knowledge about God is juxtaposed with Torah in vv. 7-14, which could separate into four sections: an introduction in praise of Torah in v. 7, an expansion of its power in vv. 8-10, a commitment by the psalmist to follow Torah in vv. 11-13, and a concluding dedication in v. 14.

Significance. These two hymns combine to celebrate God's creative handiwork and God's legal ordering of our society as distinct ways in which humans acquire knowledge of the divine. In the first hymn the message is silent or nonverbal. Here the creation speaks strongly about God's glory as it progresses through endless, repetitive cycles.

The second hymn praises the knowledge of God through Torah in six different ways: as law that is perfect (v. 7*a*), as sure decrees (v. 7*b*), as right precepts (v. 8*a*), as clear commandments (v. 8*b*), as fear of God that is pure (v. 9*a*), and, finally, as true ordinances (v. 9*b*). Each word views the Torah from a somewhat different perspective, which prompts a slightly different life-giving force: the reviving of the soul (v. 7*a*), making the simple wise (v. 7*b*), rejoicing of the heart (v. 8*a*), enlightening of the eyes (v. 8*b*), permanence in life (v. 9*a*), and, finally, righteousness (v. 9*b*). When viewed from each of the different, but related perspectives, Torah encompasses an entire world, or, to use the language from Proverbs with regard to Wisdom, a complete house. The central point in the litany of imagery, therefore, is that Torah must be viewed holistically as a complete world and life view. Verse 10 provides conclusion to this section and an introduction to the next section by introducing motive, with the claim that Torah is more desirable than gold.

Verses 11-14 pick up from v. 10 by having the psalmist enter more personally into the praise of Torah. The general statement about the universal value of Torah is now applied specifically to the speaker. ("Moreover by them is your servant warned.") After the psalmist enters personally into the praise of Torah, the overwhelming character of the law looms large momentarily, which prompts language of petition for divine grace ("Clear me of hidden faults"). The psalm ends on a personal note of dedication, not to Torah but to God, who is the source of law.

New Testament Texts

The next readings from James and Mark simply move forward in these documents, James to the next verses and Mark to the next major section of the Gospel.

The Epistle: *James 3:1-12*

The Many Meanings of a Loose Tongue

Setting. Readers may refer to the discussion of setting for Proper Seventeen for a general treatment of James. The verses of this lesson come in the final of three well-defined discourses in the central portion of the epistle. Having advocated the path of faith, perseverance, and perfection rather than that of desire, sin, and death (chapter 1), James called for an active reception of God's grace and an active life of devotion (chapter 2). Now, he returns to an idea hinted at in 1:19-20 and raised overtly in 1:26, "If any think they are religious, and do not bridle their tongues but deceive their hearts, their religion is worthless."

Structure. Commentators tend to view the passage in three parts: Verses 1-2 address those who would be teachers; vv. 3-8 are a lecture on the tongue per se; and vv. 9-12 conclude by measuring the world and the human condition in terms of the tongue's capacity for both blessing and cursing. The logic of the passage spirals. First, James calls for moderating ambitions for leadership because of the real difficulties of mastering ourselves. Then, he illustrates the danger of which we should be aware—namely, loose, damaging talk. The illustration of the potency of the tongue leads to a final movement in which James offers outright denunciation of speaking with a forked-tongue.

Significance. James reads the human condition in the context of this world, and the picture he paints is less than flattering. James's reflections are terribly embarrassing because of their accuracy, and every reader should be humbled by his candid remarks. Nevertheless, with Martin Luther who found James to be "a right strawy epistle," we may deem this revealing passage slightly short on theological profundity. Yet, there are items that point beyond the mere remarks in directions we should not miss.

The beginning and ending of this seeming diatribe on the tongue are crucial. James relates his remarks, which have great affinity with standard Hellenistic moralism about irresponsible speech, to the office of teacher in the Church. He calls for moderation in the rush to become a teacher—that is, to exercise leadership in the Church by instructing and directing others. The danger is that none of us is perfect in speech. Here, speech is nearly (perhaps is) a metaphor for human existence. The tongue is the most telling illustration of the dangers inherent in the human condition. Humans have a pronounced tendency toward hypocrisy. This is easily seen in our speech, which includes both blessing and cursing. As small as the tongue is, James illustrates well its considerable and dangerous power. By moving in the reflection to the level of blessing and cursing—two operations of the tongue, the same tongue—James brings us to view clear evidence of the cosmic struggle between good and evil. In every human life, particularly in the manner in which we humans speak, we see the conflict between God and the devil, between cosmic good and cosmic evil. The battle is real, and we humans are the arena of the strife. Our existence is full of contradictions and dangerous discrepancies, which reflect the cosmic clash of life and death. In the midst of this conflict, James calls his readers to God's side; and in the process, lest anyone underestimate the reality of the peril, James calls for modesty, which in this instance is the better part of wisdom (James's next topic in this epistle).

The passage is parenetic, not primarily theological, although there is theology implicit in this text for preachers with sufficient imagination. The grace of God directs the tongue toward blessing, away from cursing. And, the power of the tongue is a potent tool, capable of marvelous accomplishments in devotion to God's causes.

The Gospel: Mark 8:27-38

Finding What It Means to Be a Disciple

Setting. (The following discussion of setting is relevant for the next seven Sundays.) The middle portion of Mark's Gospel, from 8:22

through 10:52, contains some of the most dramatic words and events of Jesus' ministry. The section opens and closes with different stories about Jesus' healing of blind men. Commentators often describe these healings as paradigms of the faith experience of the disciples who move through the Gospel from blindness to half-sight to seeing all things clearly; and, then, after they have thrown off the mantle of their ignorance through a full encounter with the Lord, they are able to follow him in his "way." Whether this helpful, but essentially allegorical, interpretation of the boundary-stories of the middle portion of Mark is correct, it is certainly the case that Mark 8:22–10:52 contains important information about the identity of Christ and true discipleship to him. Between the two stories about blind men, there are three recognizable and repetitive cycles of material: 8:31–9:30; 9:31–10:32; 10:33-45. Though the symmetry is not perfectly patterned, in each of these sections we find (1) a Passion prediction, (2) an ensuing misunderstanding on the part of the disciples, and (3) instruction(s) by Jesus on discipleship.

Structure. Our lesson is made up of three units: the famous conversation between Jesus and the disciples at Caesarea Philippi, the first Passion prediction by Jesus, and the first instance of subsequent misunderstanding on the part of the disciples. The text as a whole presents a sharp exchange in conversation and a series of bold statements: Jesus questions; the disciples answer. Jesus questions more pointedly; Peter answers. And Jesus charges them to silence. Then, Jesus teaches. Peter attempts to rebuke him, and Jesus incontrovertibly rebukes Peter, ending the dialogue and having the final say; then, Jesus teaches. Readers are carried through this text by the vitality of the statements.

Significance. While many who encountered Jesus in his ministry were struck by his authority, there were many assessments of the significance of his words and deeds. When pressed, Jesus' closest followers could see that he was even more than most thought him to be. Peter could say he was "the Christ." But Jesus charged him to silence; it is in Matthew where Peter says even more than this and Jesus praises him. Why the command to silence? Probably because what Peter meant by *Christ* was inadequate; he likely perceived Jesus to be God's new David, a Jewish Caesar, one wielding God's power simply on this earth. Consulting a concordance will show that in Mark's use, the word *Christ* is not the central confession of who Jesus is. Above all, for Mark Jesus is "the Son of God" who came as "the Son of Man" to serve, not to be served, and to give his life for the salvation of the many. Only if *Christ* means this can it be an adequate confession; and the very next incident shows that Peter did not have an image of suffering for humankind's salvation in mind when he called Jesus the Christ. Why did Jesus tell Peter to keep quiet? To keep him from spreading bad information—right word, wrong meaning.

Jesus' foretelling of his suffering and death provokes and brings out the lack of comprehension of his disciples, in this instance Peter. How hard it is to hear about the necessity of the suffering of Christ. If Jesus is the Christ, then he should be all powerful. He should be above the fray of life in this world, and surely he should be beyond suffering. Yet, not only is he subject to the terrible forces that afflict us during life in this world, Jesus anticipates the brutal reality of tribulation and declares his commitment to experience it. And so, we can understand Peter who is shocked at what he hears and who rebukes Jesus.

The verb *to rebuke* is striking. It occurs twice in this passage, first, to state what Peter does to Jesus, and then, to describe what Jesus does to Peter. Elsewhere in Mark the verb is used to say what Jesus does to the demons he reproaches in exorcism. To rebuke is to confront and to condemn with the purpose of effecting radical change. Peter hears Jesus. Since his assumptions about the Christ were most likely colored by his time and culture, he thought of the Christ as the powerful promised heir of David. Yet, Peter finds Jesus talking about suffering and dying. Therefore, he tries to set Jesus straight.

Jesus will have none of it! "Get behind me, Satan! For you are not thinking the things of God but the things of humans." These are strange but terribly important words. The command, "get behind me," employs some of the exact words ("behind me") with which Jesus initially called Peter to discipleship (see 1:17). Jesus does not say, "Get lost!" Rather, he commands Peter to step back into the place where he called him to be—that is, into discipleship. And, that Jesus seems rude in calling Peter "Satan" is far less disturbing than the correlation between Satan and "thinking the things of humans."

The rebuke warns us that whenever we formulate plans for God, we are playing God and not being faithful.

Disciples are called to follow, not to take over the lead. To follow requires denying the self with all its selfish ambition, with its inherent resistance to God's peculiarly gracious ways. To follow means to take Jesus on his own terms and to devote ourselves at all costs to doing his will.

Proper 19: The Celebration

Today's succession of readings moves from a consideration of Wisdom and her attainment as a central concern of the religious life (Proverbs), to the application of Wisdom to the practical issues of life (James), to the Wisdom of God, which sounds like foolishness to human beings—namely, that those who seek their lives shall lose them and those who lose their lives for the sake of Christ and the gospel will save them (Mark). Paul's proclamation of Christ as "the wisdom of God" will need to be taken into consideration before preaching in order not to make a simple equation between the Wisdom figure of Proverbs and Jesus of Nazareth. This does not rule out considering how Jesus might be the embodiment of divine Wisdom.

The stanza that begins, "O come, thou wisdom from on high," from "O Come, O Come, Immanuel" may serve as a response to the Old Testament lesson. See also the Wesley hymn, "Happy Are They That Find the Grace," which is quoted under next Sunday's "Celebration" entry.

September 16 is Independence Day in Mexico. That suggests including prayers for the people and the churches of Mexico in today's intercessions. The following prayer from Mexico, with its reference to our foolishness, may be used somewhere in the service, printed in the bulletin, or used in the sermon:

> Lord,
> if this day you have to correct us,
> put us right not out of anger
> but with a mother and father's love.
> So may we your children
> be kept free of falseness and foolishness.

(John Carden, ed., *With All God's People: The New Ecumenical Prayer Cycle* [Geneva: WCC, 1989], p. 261)

The concluding verse of today's psalm is frequently used by preachers immediately before the sermon, with the change of "my heart" to "our hearts." That brings up the question of the appropriateness of a public prayer immediately before the preaching of the sermon. Arguments could be made on either side of the case, but there ought to be general agreement that if prayer is offered, it will not be an occasion for the preacher to do the praying that should have been done earlier in the study; the congregation should not be expected to listen in on the preacher's private devotions. Prayers that describe the preacher's emotional and spiritual state are in questionable taste and give the impression that the preacher is more concerned with getting on the right side of the congregation than addressing God. If prayer is offered immediately prior to the sermon by the preacher, it should be from the same stance in which all pastoral prayer is offered, as that of one person chosen by the congregation to give voice to their shared aspirations.

Hymns appropriate to the Gospel lesson are " 'Take Up Your Cross,' the Savior Said," "Must Jesus Bear the Cross Alone," and "Am I a Soldier of the Cross."

Proper Twenty
Sunday Between September
18 and 24 Inclusive

Old Testament Texts

Proverbs 31:10-31 lists the characteristics of the ideal wife. Psalm 1 is a wisdom psalm.

The Lesson: *Proverbs 31:10-31*

Wisdom as Wife

Setting. Proverbs 31:10-31 reads as though it could have been a lead article in *Time* magazine about the plight of the contemporary woman. There is nothing that she can't do superbly all of the time at the same time. Is this text in fact about a superwoman? As you might expect, there is debate on this point. Proverbs 31:1-31 is the concluding section to the book, and it begins with its own superscription. The speaker of this section is a woman—the mother of King Lemuel. The chapter appears to be her advice, first, concerning her son's role as king in vv. 1-9 (he must remain focused on caring for the poor and needy), and, second, concerning the kind of woman he should marry in vv. 10-31 (presumably to accomplish the goal of caring for the poor and needy). Is this in fact a practical check list for marriage? If so, it is either a male fantasy or a nightmare, depending on the self-image of the potential groom. When one views the variety of activities of this potential bride, one suspects that the subject matter is actually the woman, Wisdom, and that the check list is a sketch of the kind of practical activities that she is able to influence if one enters her house, feasts with her (9:1-6), and, in the end, marries her (31:10-31).

Structure. As noted Proverbs 31 breaks into two parts, which should not be separated from each other. The advice about avoiding a life-style of womanizing (v. 3) and excessive partying (vv. 4-5) and, instead, focusing on the needs of the poor must be seen as the backdrop for the soliloquy on the perfect wife (vv. 10-31). The latter text is difficult to break into small units because it is structured as an acrostic (each line of vv. 10-31 begins with a letter of the Hebrew alphabet). In view of this it is probably better to interpret the list of characteristics of Wisdom as a whole and not seek to break them into smaller parts.

Significance. What does the perfect wife do? She makes her own clothes (v. 13), does all the cooking (v. 14), manages the household (v. 15), dabbles in real estate (v. 16), has an interest in commerce (v. 18), is involved in manufacturing (vv. 19, 24), works in social services (v. 20), can handle unexpected tragedies due to snow in the desert (v. 21), is the power behind her husband's success (v. 21), possesses prophetic clairvoyance (v. 25), provides home education for her children (v. 26), never watches television (v. 27), is the perfect mother and wife (v. 28), and, finally, goes to church regularly (v. 30).

Who is the perfect wife? Clearly it is the woman Wisdom and her activity is nothing less than the management of an entire country both with regard to its internal social structure and its international political relationships. Wisdom has been personified throughout the book of Proverbs. Her personality, however, has been mythic in proportions. She was with God at the outset of creation and his darling (Proverbs 8). In her other appearances writers have underscored that she must not be admired from a distance. Even though Wisdom has divine power, she wishes to be active in our everyday lives. Proverbs 1:20-31 provides an example of this, when Wisdom is placed in the midst of the marketplace and pictured as calling out to people in their everyday activity. Yet even here she is extraordinary in power. Her authority is clearly divine and her powers were more prophetic than mundane. The conclusion of the book of Proverbs goes a step further by pulling Wisdom even more intimately into the everyday affairs of humans by making her the wife of the king and then showing what she can do in all aspects of mundane life as the real power behind the monarch.

The larger setting of Proverbs 31 is important for preaching. The advice of Lemuel's mother is described as an oracle ("An oracle that his mother taught him"). What this signals is that the litany of Wisdom as the perfect wife is prophetic insight. It is not simply academic knowledge, learned in the classroom. It is revelation, that once learned, must be applied to all aspects of life. Thus the book ends by personifying Wisdom into the most intimate setting of all—as wife. And her power is illustrated in the most mundane ways possible, by listing specific activities that are done by real people in real situations. The effect of these varied activities, however, when viewed collectively, is no less stunning than the earlier idealizations of Wisdom as a divine force in creation and as prophet in the marketplace.

The Response: *Psalm 1*

Two Ways

Setting. Psalm 1 is a powerful example of didactic poetry in the psalter. Its language is reminiscent of Proverbs. The clear indications of influence from the Wisdom tradition in this psalm, as well as its apparent absence in early numbering systems of the psalms (the Western text of Acts 13:33 quotes Psalm 2 as being Psalm 1), have prompted scholars to argue that Psalm 1 is meant to function as an introduction to the entire psalter. The psalm, therefore, may never have been intended to have a cultic setting for its use, but as providing a perspective in which to read the entire book of Psalms. The heading "two ways" arises from the sharp contrast in v. 6 between the "way of the righteous" and the "way of the wicked."

Structure. The contrast between the righteous and the wicked stated so sharply in v. 6 is central to the structure of the entire psalm. Verses 1-3 describe the way of the righteous, while vv. 4-5 (or 6 if it is not read as a concluding summary) provide contrast by describing the fate of the wicked.

Significance. Who are the righteous? They are first described in v. 2 by what they do not do. Notice the three verbs here, which follow a certain progression. The righteous (1) do not follow, (2) do not take the path, and (3) do not sit in the seat of wicked persons, sinners, scoffers. Then what do they do? The righteous evince a constancy in life that is predictable because they have internalized Torah (v. 2). Thus, they are equipped for the long haul in life, and the writer underscores this point by introducing the motif of a tree with deep roots planted by a stream (v. 3). The wicked, by contrast, have no roots. Consequently, they blow with the wind (v. 4).

The point of this psalm is not simply legalism. Torah in v. 2 is being understood in this context not only as Scripture, but even more as God's moral structure for the world, which is able to provide meaning to human action for anyone who chooses to enter into it. Torah and Wisdom overlap at this point, since both are essential for structuring meaningful human action. The wicked person is one who rejects the structure of God's world. The psalm is an introduction to the psalter, because this insight about the necessity of entering God's world of Torah (or of entering Wisdom's house as in Proverbs 9:1-6) is a prerequisite for making all the language of the psalms meaningful.

New Testament Texts

The lessons are both sets of instruction on the nature of Christian discipleship. James charges his readers directly about the manner of Christian life, whereas Mark recalls events from the ministry that lead to statements by Jesus to his followers (and, subsequently to readers) about the character of true discipleship.

The Epistle: *James 3:13–4:3, 7-8a*

Preferring God and God's Wisdom over the Devil and Devilish Ways

Setting. Commentators regard 3:13–5:20 as loosely structured parenetic materials, none of which is so tightly organized as the set of discourses in 2:1–3:12; yet, within this body of practical instructions there are sections with discernible catchwords and concerns. The verses of our lesson come from a section, 3:13–4:10, that interpreters refer to as meditations on friendship with God. Unfortunately, the selected verses of the lesson omit the lines that use the metaphor of friendship, though the basic flow of the author's thought is preserved in the suggested reading.

Structure. Verses 13-18 of chapter 3 praise wisdom "come down from above" which yields "a harvest of righteousness . . . in peace" and denounce the opposite, "earthly, unspiritual, and devilish" wisdom, which is "boastful and false to the truth." Having raised the issue of devilish wisdom, James turns to his audience in 4:1-3, again recognizing the war of forces within them. In the verses omitted from the lesson (4:4-6) James denounces "friendship with the world," which he labels as "enmity with God." Then, in the final verses of our lesson, 7-8*a*, James instructs his readers to action: They are to submit to God and resist the devil. He promises that if they draw near to God that God will draw near to them. Thus, in four movements James (1) ponders the options for life available to believers, (2) examines the genuine difficulty faced for living rightly, (3) calls for active resistance and submission, and (4) promises God's presence and aid (as becomes clear in 4:10).

Significance. The line of thought in the lesson suggests the shape and the content of a sermon on this text. Yet, from the outset we must be vigilant lest we lapse into mere moralism or pious drivel. James's ancient rhetoric meets our modern cause-and-effect minds and tempts us to squeeze a "do-and-don't" list or a formula for reaping the benefits of righteousness from this passage. The text, however, is actually about a way of life that grows out of one kind of relationship with God rather than another kind of life that results from the wrong involvements. If we read James carefully, we see that he does not say that if we do "A" we will end up in God's good graces, but if we do "B" we will end up in cahoots with the devil. Rather, James argues that we lead different styles of life because of the primary relationships we form.

James makes observations about different kinds of living in order (1) to advocate that the readers submit themselves to God and (2) to admonish them to resist the devil. His logic, however, is inductive, not deductive. In this light, the final lines in our lesson, "Draw near to God, and he will draw near to you," are a promise about a relationship that effects a life "full of mercy and good fruits, without a trace of partiality or hypocrisy." There are at least two important implications in the argument that James mounts. First, human beings have responsibility and genuine options concerning the character of their lives. And, although James can appear somewhat negative in his remarks, we should see that he does not minimize the difficulties inherent in human life. The picture James paints is not meant as a scare tactic. James simply states his convictions and perceptions about the human condition and the reality of life. Second, James's message is, above all, good news. Humans are not simply set in the world and left to their own devices. God is present as our companion—not our copilot or other images from bumper stickers—rather, as v. 5 says, ''God yearns jealously for the spirit that he has made to dwell in us.'' God is intimately involved in our living, and if we live faithfully in relationship to God, we have the assurance that God draws near (nearer!) to us.

The Gospel: *Mark 9:30-37*

Greatness According to God's Grace

Setting. Readers may refer to the discussion of setting for the Gospel lesson for Proper Nineteen for observations about the general section of Mark in which this week's lesson occurs. Specifically our lesson comes in the second of three cycles of prophecy, misunderstanding, and teaching related to Jesus' dramatic predictions of his forthcoming Passion, death, and resurrection.

Structure. The lesson has two distinct and highly related parts. First, we read about the misunderstanding or lack of comprehension among the disciples (vv. 33-34) after Jesus uttered the second of his Passion predictions (9:31-32); and, then, Mark records Jesus' words of correction and further instruction in response to the disciples' misperception of their status. Though the sections are distinguishable and capable of standing independently, together they form a powerful lesson that invites us genuinely to engage Mark's material.

Significance. Last week we saw how Simon Peter failed to grasp the teaching of Jesus about who Jesus was and what it means to be his disciple. Now, we come to another moment in the ministry of Jesus where all his disciples miss the point of his teaching and misconstrue what it means to be called to follow him.

Our lesson begins immediately after Jesus speaks of his suffering, death, and resurrection. It is crucial to notice the relationship of the incidents recorded in our lesson with Jesus' foregoing statement. Indeed, Mark tells the reader in 9:32 that "they did not understand what he was saying and were afraid to ask him." This remark informs us of the hesitating ignorance of the disciples and tells us how to frame their debate about greatness. The disciples hear Jesus. They do not comprehend. They are too inhibited to ask for clarification, but they go ahead to a discussion they formulated—a discussion that seems to occupy them at length and in earnest, a discussion that gets at the heart of their understanding of Christian discipleship, namely, a discussion of who was the greatest. The contrast with their previously acknowledged lack of understanding would be comical if it were not so sad. Jesus calls them to follow, and they think of greatness. Jesus speaks of his own suffering and dying, even of his resurrection; but they argue about who among them is the greatest. Clearly the disciples comprehend their calling as an opportunity for privilege, power, and position. For these disciples, discipleship means service, but service to them. The last thing they think of as they discuss their relative positions in Jesus' band of followers is the kind of sacrificial outpouring of self that Jesus points to in referring to his Passion.

Before we get carried away with denouncing the disciples, it may be well to ponder our own reasons for following Christ. In a world in love with itself where we are told that it's okay, indeed that it's great, to promote ourselves, the disciples look pretty normal. Lack of ambition is suspect, perhaps an indication that one is not psychologically healthy; so what's wrong with the disciples? A poll of tithers in a mainstream denomination revealed that 90 percent of those who gave expected to get something in return. They mentioned snappy sermons, rousing choral anthems, smooth pastoral calling, and a full range of programs for the family. Very few spoke of service, and no one mentioned suffering.

The miscomprehension—or, better, the total lack of understanding—of the disciples invites further teaching from Jesus. He begins by telling them that if they want to be first, they must be last. Specifically, they must be servants of all. His directions surely seemed odd, for they completely reverse this world's standards. Greatness, says Jesus, is measured by what you do for others, not by achieving a superior position in life that will ensure getting service from others. In this world Jesus sounds like a madman. Why believe what he says? The fact is in this world those who hold the reins of power and the purse strings of economic well-being look pretty great and seem to have it pretty good. So, why believe Jesus? It is a reasonable, natural, even necessary question.

Jesus has an answer. It comes in a picture lesson. He set a child among them. It is easy for us to misperceive Jesus' message. In our world, where children are the apples of their parents' eyes, the virtual princes and princesses of the family, we are apt to miss Jesus' point. In the Greco-Roman world, including the Jews, children were thought of as unbridled little bits of chaos. They were not considered naive, innocent, sweet, and trusting; ancients regarded children as terrible nuisances who were to be disciplined and tolerated until they became useful, reasonable adults. In Greco-Roman culture children were without status, and they possessed no power to give them position. There was no profit in taking in such (temporarily) useless people.

Jesus says, "Whoever welcomes one such child in my name welcomes me, and whoever welcomes me welcomes not me but the one who sent me." What does this mean? God in Jesus Christ demonstrates gracious acceptance of humans who have nothing about them to lay a claim on God's generosity; but it is the character of God to be gracious. Thus, God gives service to all, despite their absolute inability to do anything for God's benefit. Jesus says people who treat others as God treats them are great. Why? Because they live like God, and God is great.

Proper 20: The Celebration

The pattern we observed last Sunday between the lessons pertains today, as well. The description of the woman Wisdom in Proverbs 31 finds application in daily living in James, and in Mark is embodied in the work and words of Jesus concerning life in the new age that his ministry inaugurates.

The following passage from *The Prayers and Meditations of St. Anselm* (1033–1109; Archbishop of Canterbury 1093–1109) illustrates that there is a tradition of characterizing Christ as a mother going back into the Middle Ages. This may be helpful if the preacher intends to deal in any way with the identification of Sophia or Wisdom as the Second Person of the Trinity. In the same way, the use of children and the meaning of greatness in the Gospel reading may be related to this selection from Anselm.

> And you, Jesus, are you not also a mother?
> Are you not the mother who, like a hen,
> gathers her chickens under her wings?
> Truly, Lord, you are a mother;
> for both they who are in labour
> and they who are brought forth
> are accepted by you.
> You have died more than they, that they may labour to bear.
> It is by your death that they have been born,
> for if you had not been in labour,
> you could not have borne death;
> and if you had not died, you would not have brought forth.
> For, longing to bear sons into life,
> you tasted of death,
> and by dying you begot them.
> You did this in your own self,
> your servants by your commands and help.
> You as the author, they as the ministers.
> So you, Lord God, are the great mother.

(*The Prayers and Meditations of Saint Anselm*, Sister Benedicta Ward, S.L.G., trans. [Harmondsworth, Middlesex, England: Penguin Books, 1973], pp. 153-54)

The following stanzas from Charles Wesley are a fitting connection between the epistle and Gospel readings.

> Happy are they that find the grace,
> the blessing of God's chosen race,
> the wisdom coming from above,
> the faith that sweetly works by love.

> Wisdom divine! Who tells the price
> of wisdom's costly merchandise?
> Wisdom to silver we prefer,
> and gold is dross compared to her.

> Her hands are filled with length of days,
> true riches, and immortal praise,
> riches of Christ, on all bestowed,
> and honor that descends from God.

To purest joys she all invites,
chaste, holy, spiritual delights;
her ways are ways of pleasantness,
and all her flowery paths are peace.

Happy are they who wisdom gain,
thrice happy who their guest retain;
they own, and shall for ever own,
wisdom, and Christ, and heaven are one.

Long meter tunes such as Hursley, Melcombe, Pentecost, or Wareham are appropriate.

The first stanza of "Take Time to Be Holy" is another suggested response to the epistle reading. The whole hymn could be used if desired.

Proper Twenty-one
Sunday Between September 25 and October 1 Inclusive

Old Testament Texts

Esther 7:1-6, 9-10; 9:20-22 describes the inauguration of the festival of Purim. Psalm 124 is a hymn of thanksgiving.

The Lesson: *Esther 7:1-6, 9-10; 9:20-22*

Chance and Providence

Setting. The festival of Purim requires a word of explanation, since it is a religious holiday that has not continued in Christian tradition. Purim comes from the Hebrew word *pur*, meaning "lot" as in the casting of lots. Thus the Jewish festival of Purim would appear to address issues of fate and destiny in some form, on which the story of Esther is meant to illustrate or provide commentary. Purim is a two-day festival, which in the story of Esther occurs on the fourteenth and fifteenth days of Adar (the last month of the year corresponding to February-March in our present calendrical system). The reason for these dates is given in the story. Haman, the evil protagonist who was jealous of Mordecai, sought to have all the Jews killed on the thirteenth day of Adar through a decree of King Ahasuerus. The plot structure of the story shows how Haman was eventually killed and how Esther and Mordecai influenced the king to make a new decree that all Jews could defend themselves against their enemies on the thirteenth day of Adar. Purim is a joyous celebration of life and rest on the two days after this day of defense, when gifts are exchanged. Note how the two-day sequence of the festival is ironically built into the story in chapters 5–7, when Esther invites King Ahasuerus and Haman to a two-day festival in her house, which results in the downfall of the evil Haman. A careful reading of the book will bring to light many more correlations between the narrative and the festival of Purim.

Structure. Twice in the story, Queen Esther risks her life to save the Jews by approaching King Ahasuerus without being requested: the first instance includes chapters 5–7, and the second, chapters 8–9. The two lectionary texts can be read as providing concluding episodes to each of these two actions of Esther. Chapter 7:1-6, 9-10 concludes the account of Esther's two-day banquet for King Ahasuerus and Haman, which began in chapter 5 when Esther risked her life to approach King Ahasuerus in order to request his presence at her home. Chapter 7:1-6 is the account of Esther pleading that the king save all Jews in the kingdom from the plotting of Haman. The request is news to the king, who then kills Haman for plotting such a thing. Chapter 9:20-22 describes the actual celebration of Purim, which is the result of Esther's second approach to the king in 8:3-8. The killing of Haman did not really solve the problem for the Jews because a decree from the king had already gone out that all Jews could be killed on the thirteenth of Adar. The decree is fate and cannot be withdrawn, but the king supplements this decree with another, that all Jews can defend themselves against their enemies on this day. Chapter 9:20-22 describes how the Jews celebrated Purim on the fourteenth and fifteenth of Adar after destroying 75,000 of their enemies on the thirteenth day.

Significance. Esther is too often overlooked in the Christian tradition, or if it is read, it is interpreted only politically, as a tract that was meant to support patriotism in the Maccabean era (second century B.C.E.). In support of this conclusion, writers are quick to underscore the complete absence of any references to God in the book. All biblical books have social and political aims embedded in their composition, and the book of Esther is no different. All biblical books also have a theological message, and this includes the book of Esther. The absence of God in the story is the key for preaching this book. The reader is given no easy clues to uncover divine action or motive in the events of the book of Esther.

No prophets enter the story to tell us what God is thinking, and there is not an omniscient narrator to link heaven and earth for us. Instead, we are only allowed to see raw events unfold before us. In addition, an emphasis on fate throughout the book further accentuates the lack of reference to God. The plot begins with a concept of fate in 3:7-15. The casting of a lot prompts Haman to influence a monarchical decree against the Jews. There is a certain arbitrariness in whether the king would approve or disapprove of the approach of Esther. Then, too, Haman's well-conceived plans also unwind in an arbitrary way. Just when he believes that he is reaching the nadir of power, the king has a dream and honors Mordecai, the very person for whom he is building a gallows upon which to hang. The next day Haman dies on the gallows he built for Mordecai.

The book of Esther is about chance, ambiguity, and providence. God is kept out of the story for the simple reason that God is both absent and present in all of these events, and that to single out a divine character as one among many would take away from the power of the story. A confession of divine providence lacks the clarity of prophetic speech. Consequently it requires risky action even when we lack the moral clarity of knowing exactly how God is acting in the situation.

Two characters in the book capture the religious perspective of confessing providence, even when God is lost in the background. The first is negative. It is Haman's wife, Zeresh, in 6:13, who counsels her husband about Mordecai after the king's dream: "If Mordecai, before whom your downfall has begun, is of the Jewish people, you will not prevail against him, but will surely fall before him." Her intuitions are in fact prophetic, since her husband is hung the next day. The effect of her words is that they cast a spell over the plot by suggesting a larger design to these events than even the crafty Haman may have imagined. The second example is positive. In 4:14 Mordecai sends a message to Esther, encouraging her to risk her position to help the Jewish people. He concludes his message with a tentative confession of providence: "Who knows? Perhaps you have come to royal dignity for just such a time as this." These words grasp the heart of a confession of providence. There is no direct word from God. There is no active divine character to confirm the risk taking. Instead, there is only a tentative confession that is stated in the subjunctive. Take the risk, it may be why your life has gone the way that it has. The power of providence is not first and foremost in our analysis of events safely after the fact. The power of providence is our tentative confession of God at the outset of life-threatening events, when there is not clarity.

The Response: *Psalm 124*

A Hymn of Thanksgiving

Setting. Psalm 124 is unusual because it is presented as being a thanksgiving of the community. Such national songs of thanksgiving are rare when compared to individual songs of thanksgiving, which presents a range of form-critical problems about the origin and use of this psalm. In any case the psalm appears to have borrowed language from the individual songs of thanksgiving in order to become a prayer of instruction aimed at helping people gain insight into divine help.

Structure. Psalm 124 separates into two or three sections. Verses 1-5 provide an introduction to the psalm. Here the people of Israel are encouraged, and, indeed, instructed with very specific language to praise God. Verses 6-7 contain the actual praise of God with v. 8 either continuing the praise or providing a conclusion.

Significance. The significance of Psalm 124, when it is read in the context of Esther, is that it supplies the language of praise for divine providence or rescue in a threatening situation; the book of Esther lacks language of this kind. The introduction sketches out in vv. 3-5 (note the three instances of *then*) what the fateful possibilities might have been for the people of God without the help of God. Verse 6 turns the direction of the psalm by stating the actual thanksgiving, while v. 7 provides a contrasting picture of Israel from vv. 3-5, as a bird escaping from a trap. Verse 8 provides an appropriate conclusion in light of the event of rescue. Help does indeed come from God the creator.

New Testament Texts

Both lessons bring together a series of statements giving practical instructions about the nature of life in the community of faith. James's remarks are all positive directions in relation to difficulties faced by members of the congregation. Jesus' teachings in Mark also direct the disciples to action, but there is an undertone of warning that calls for real discipline in living the life of faith.

The Epistle: *James 5:13-20*

Compassion and Prayer in the Christian Community

Setting. Beginning with the twelfth verse of chapter 5 and running to the end of the epistle, James assembles a series of individual exhortations about the way believers are to go about living together as members of a congregation. The so-called letter has an epistolary-style beginning, but there is nothing else in the writing that resembles a letter. Thus, as we come to the end of James there is neither a final greeting nor a closing statement. Instead, the concluding cluster of parenetic remarks simply ends.

Structure. In these last directions James tells his readers how to deal with those who are ill among them (vv. 13-16a). One thing that is especially important to do when there are sick persons is to pray for them. Calling for prayer for the sick, in turn, leads to comments about the power of prayer (vv. 16b-18). Finally, vv. 19-20 remind the readers of the importance of their mutual concern, care, and correction of one another—perhaps the most crucial function of the life of a congregation.

James's thought here runs from caring for the sick to the power of prayer to caring for and correcting those who stray from the truth. The direction of his reflection may well be deliberate, for James begins and ends with observations about caring for others—first, those with explicit physical (and implicit spiritual?) needs, and second, those with explicit spiritual difficulties. Between these comments James sandwiches declarations about the efficacy of prayer. While prayer is obviously related to this issue of caring for the ill, it precedes and probably leads to the matter of caring for those who wander from the truth, so that prayer is a crucial ingredient in vital aspects of Christian communal life.

Significance. James declares that the members of the Christian community are to care for one another in every way. Believers are to attend to one another both physically and spiritually. The call into the community of faith is a call into a corporate life wherein our relationships with one another are complex and concerned with every aspect of living. James anticipates that among the members of a Christian congregation there will be mutual acts of kindness, words of assurance, and even caring correction of those whose lives go astray.

The ultimate source for this community life characterized by compassion, certitude, and comfort is the vital relationship of each and every member to God. Thus, James writes about a life of prayer, praise, and confession—that is, activities that bind the community together as the lives of the members are mutually oriented toward God. A life of piety and devotion to God finds expression in the activities of caring for the sick, praying for one another, and bringing back those who wander from the truth.

We can view this passage as a fairly abstract call for concern, stated in spiritual terms. But, as we think about James's directions, his words call us through genuine piety into the hard work of being a Christian congregation. As believers belonging to a congregation we may worship together, we may study together, and we may take on worthy projects together; but the form of life that James envisions goes beyond the shape of typical twentieth-century congregational life to address some of the most personal portions of our lives. Some few members of every congregation are actively involved with the care of the sick, but are the majority comfortable with such expressions and acts of concern? Fewer still are active in efforts to bring back those who seem to be wandering from the truth. Who are we to define truth? Who are we to invade the privacy of others? Who are we to suggest to others the errors of their ways and to call on them to return to the truth of Christian faith? We live private, seemingly sensitive lives wherein we seek to honor the freedom and independence of others.

Yet, as James would see it there is little concern or risk in our approach. James calls us all to prayer. The fact is we do not define the truth and we do not have the right to impose ourselves and our views on others. But as God's people we live under the Lordship of God and we have the responsibility, not the right, to exercise Christian concern at every level. James tells us plainly that we always do this through prayer under the direction of God.

The Gospel: *Mark 9:38-50*

Discipleship as Devotion to Doing God's Will

Setting. Our lesson comes again from the second of the three cycles of prophecy, misunderstanding, and subsequent teaching. Jesus foretells his pending Passion, his disciples fail to understand, and Jesus offers initial correcting instruction. Then, we come to a section of material that gives his followers additional, more elaborate direction about the life of discipleship. This material begins in 9:38 and continues through 10:31.

Structure. Two blocks of very distinct materials form our lesson. First, in vv. 38-41, there is a discussion provoked by the disciples' reaction to an exorcist, not a follower, who casts out demons in Jesus' name. The thrust of this section is to define who forms the "in group" related to Jesus. Second, vv. 42-50 collect statements declaring that true disciples do God's will at all costs. There is some relationship between these units, though they are not necessarily related. One may elect to deal with one or both of the sections.

Significance. The story and dialogue in vv. 38-41 show a sharp contrast between the attitude of the disciples (as seen in John's report) and the attitude of Jesus (shown in his statements here). The disciples want a careful, restrictive definition of appropriate action in the name of Jesus Christ. They contend for a conservative, constricting specificity: Only authorized activity is to be allowed. Jesus, on the other hand, is not so strict. He declares that God's work done in his name is to be honored, not scrutinized for credentials. Jesus' principle is to include, not to exclude. He says, "Whoever is not against us is for us." (It is in Matthew 12:30, in a completely different set of circumstances that we find Jesus saying, "Whoever is not with me is against me, and whoever does not gather with me scatters.") Jesus' words may make us nervous. Where is the control here? But notice that his comment is in relation to active work in his name that does not come under his overseeing; he is not commenting on any and all activity. If healing is being done in his name but apart from his supervision, then Jesus accepts the authenticity of the work. He taught that his own power was God's, so if one who is not among his immediate followers is busy with the same work he does and even does it in his name, then Jesus judges that one to be doing God's work. For us this may mean that a religious rulebook or a statement of denominational polity may ultimately prove inadequate to assess the validity of active Christian ministry. The verification of the work of God requires the discernment of the living Spirit of God, for God's work is itself living, fresh, and capable of surprises. Jesus' concluding words about the cup of water given because of "the name of Christ" indicates that no one who acknowledges him is to be scorned. Indeed, God's work in Christ's name is not only to be allowed, it will bring reward.

In vv. 42-50 we come to a combination of materials. At times the motive for the combinations are apparent, but at others the reasons these sayings are brought together are not entirely clear. Verses 42-48 illustrate a theme: If anything causes you to sin, do away with it at all costs. Verse 49 follows, apparently linked to the previous lines by the word fire, yet referring to the action of salting; and then, v. 50 is joined to the section because of its metaphorical discussion of salt. This combination is strange, operating loosely through catchwords; but the sense of the statements is quite clear. The entire section is metaphorical and hyperbolic—that is, it employs striking, poetic images that exaggerate in order to communicate in an effective and memorable way.

Together the verses of the lesson form the following crucial but prosaic message: A radical concern with God and with God's own concerns is the key to fellowship with God, and such a relationship is so important that nothing must hinder it. Any hindrance is to be eliminated. Indeed, every human life will be evaluated in terms of a vital relationship to God. Moreover, the value of a vital relationship to God has to do with more than final judgment. When our lives are bound up with God, we humans have a quality of life in relationship to one another that transcends mere earthly standards and manifests God's peace. This message is vital and true, but Jesus' dramatic metaphors make the meaning memorable as well as plain. Preachers should take a cue from Jesus here. Find striking images, metaphors, and stories to communicate this gospel message.

Proper 21: The Celebration

The appearance of the name *Ahasuerus* in today's Old Testament lesson reminds me of an experience as a guest preacher when the host pastor stood up to read the scripture lesson from the beginning of the book of Ruth and was confronted with the names of Elimelech, Mahlon, and Chilion. After a couple of disastrous attempts to get his tongue around them, he turned to me and said, "I guess I should have looked at this earlier." That said much more to the congregation about the reverence (or lack thereof) that he had toward the scriptures than any number of sermons might have done. He did not think the public reading of the Bible was important enough to prepare for it.

Contrast that shoddy work with the reverence demonstrated toward the Torah in the synagogue service, or with the reading of the book of Esther on the feast of Purim. As the scroll is opened, the congregation sings, "We praise You, O God, Sovereign of existence, who has hallowed our lives with commandments and commanded us to read this scroll" (*The Five Scrolls* [New York: Central Conference of American Rabbis, 1984], p. 86). This could serve as a response to the reading of this lesson today.

The worship committee might wish to consider how effectively the volume of the scriptures is being used symbolically in your church's liturgy. What does it mean to have an antiquated pulpit Bible in the King James version sitting ignored on the communion table on a missal stand too small for it, while the lessons are read from individual Bibles brought forward by readers or from looseleaf inserts in the bulletin? Has the Bible become an empty symbol in that setting? Contrast that with the solemn entrance of the sacred book at the beginning of the service, its reverent "enthronement" and opening on the lectern or pulpit, and its actual use as the volume from which the lessons are read. An unused Bible sitting on the communion table where the communion elements ought to be is to mix symbols, so that neither makes a clear statement in its own right.

The plight of the Jews in Esther suggests that today's intercessions should recall both the holocaust and those who live under the threat of racial hatred and genocide.

The lesson from James is the classical scriptural warrant for the anointing of the sick and can provide an opportunity to discuss the Church's ministry of healing. There is a sense in which every sacrament or sacramental act is a commentary on and a renewing of our baptism, the sacrament of initiation. In baptism we have been delivered from the sickness of sin and the power of death in the washing with water and anointing with oil, which makes us a part of the royal priesthood. The anointing of the sick is intended to stir up within us a dynamic remembrance that we have been delivered from the power of death and so may walk through the valley of the shadow without fear. Increasingly, Protestant denominations are making available forms for the use of the anointing of the sick. Suggested resources include *Occasional Services: A Companion to the Lutheran Book of Worship* (Minneapolis, 1982), pp. 89-102; the Church of the Brethren's *Pastor's Manual* (Elgin, Ill., 1978), pp. 63-71; the Episcopal Church's *Book of Occasional Services* (New York, 1979), pp. 147-54; the Presbyterian Church's *Services for Occasions of Pastoral Care: Supplemental Liturgical Resource*, 6 (Louisville, 1990), pp. 118-20, and the United Methodist *Book of Worship* (Nashville, 1992), pp. 613-29.

Mark 9:41 is reflected in the great social gospel hymn, "Where Cross the Crowded Ways of Life," in the stanza beginning, "The cup of water given for you."

Proper Twenty-two
Sunday Between October
2 and 8 Inclusive

Old Testament Texts

Job 1:1; 2:1-10 is part of the prologue to the book of Job and emphasizes Job's moral integrity. Psalm 26 is a lament psalm that emphasizes the moral integrity of a suffering individual.

The Lesson: *Job 1:1; 2:1-10*

Doubts About God

Setting. The next four lectionary texts come from the book of Job. The very mention of the book prompts images of human suffering. A quick glance at even an abridged dictionary illustrates how the book has infiltrated our cultural consciousness: Job is "the hero of an Old Testament book who endures afflictions with fortitude and faith''; the phrase, *Job's comforter,* is "one who discourages or depresses while seemingly giving comfort and consolation''; while *Job's tears* signify "hard pearly white seeds often used as beads." The Hebrew name for Job may in fact mean "the hated or persecuted one," or perhaps an invocation, "Where is the divine father?" (*'ayya-'abun*). The two possible meanings of the name Job illustrate, first, how Job and suffering are nearly synonymous, and, second, how this close relationship demands our attention from two perspectives—the human (Job on earth) and the divine (God in heaven).

The problem of suffering takes on a somewhat different form when viewed from the distinct perspectives of God and Job. What is similar from either perspective, however, is that the threat which suffering possesses can only be overcome by whatever party is not the primary focus of interpretation. In other words, God needs Job and Job needs God to overcome the accusation of the Satan. What makes this interdependency all the more powerful is that neither God nor Job talk directly with each other for most of the book. Consequently they must trust each other in silence. When we read the story with a focus on Job, the book probes suffering from an existential point of view, which ultimately forces us to raise questions of divine motive, which can give rise to a problem of theodicy—namely, the relationship between divine power and the existence of evil, especially when there is unjust suffering. Theodicy is frequently the central topic throughout the dialogue between Job and his comforters (the speeches in chapters 3–37). The prologue to the book of Job (chapters 1–2), which is the lectionary text for this week, focuses on God and God's dependence on Job to overcome the accusation of the Satan, by exploring human motivation.

Structure. Job 1–2 consists of an introduction (1:1-5), followed by two cycles of action, which are a repetition of each other (cycle one includes 1:6-22 and cycle two includes 2:1-10), and it ends with a conclusion in 2:11-13. This brief overview of the prologue illustrates how the lectionary text includes the opening verse of the introduction (1:1), and the second of the two cycles of action (2:1-10). An essential insight for interpreting both the prologue and the book of Job as a whole is to note how heaven and earth are carefully separated. Each of the first two cycles is clearly divided between a scene in heaven with God and other divine beings (cycle one in 1:6-12 and cycle two in 2:1-7*a*) and a subsequent scene on earth with Job and other humans (cycle one in 1:13-22 and cycle two in 2:7*b*-10). The importance of these two distinct settings cannot be overemphasized. Throughout the book of Job the reader must remember that God is in heaven and Job is on earth, and, that in spite of Job's vast talk about God and God's brief assessment of Job, for the most part neither character talks directly to the other, even though the speech of each indicates their mutual dependence.

The character that links the two settings in the book is the Satan, who is one of the sons of God (Hebrew, *bene ha'elohim*, translated in the NRSV as, "heavenly beings"). He roams both earth and heaven. The name *Satan* means "accuser" in Hebrew and that is his role in the story. The imagery of the prologue is of a divine court in heaven, in which the Lord is the ruler and minor deities present themselves before the king. The Satan is presented as the voice of doubt, which finds expression in accusation. Our interpretation of Job 1:1; 2:1-10 will focus on this setting. The central problem, therefore, is to determine what it is that the Accuser doubts about God.

Significance. Job 2:1-10 separates into three parts: the opening divine challenge in vv. 1-3; the Satan's counter-challenge in v. 4; and the test along with Job's initial response in vv. 5-10.

The opening divine challenge (2:1-3). Notice that in both of the heavenly scenes in the prologue it is God who initiates the controversy with the Accuser. In Job 1:8 God states to the Satan after hearing that he has been roaming the earth: "Have you considered my servant Job? There is no one like him on earth, a blameless and upright man who fears God and turns away from evil." This divine challenge is extended in the lectionary text of 2:3 with the addition: "He still persists in his integrity, although you incited me against him to destroy him for no reason." God's challenge to the Satan is that Job is genuinely good, a person of integrity (Hebrew, *tam,* meaning "complete, right, wholesome"; and *yašar,* meaning "straight, smooth, level"—hence "upright, just"), whose fear of God and upright life-style are pure in motive, an end unto themselves. Simply stated, God's challenge to the Satan is that Job is not only good, but that he loves to be good. Hence it is a challenge that goes beyond action to motivation. The extent of this challenge must be illustrated in preaching this text, for it underscores the importance of Job in confirming the truth of the divine statement. Statements about the actions of others are controllable if the speaker has enough power, since it is possible to force our will on others. Statements about motivation, however, always go beyond the control of the speaker. Yet it is here that we must interpret the divine claim in 1:8 and 2:3. God's challenge to the Satan goes beyond action to include motive: Job is not only good, he loves goodness. The divine claim is not about God but about the effectiveness of God on humanity, which raises the question: Can humans be transformed to love goodness as an end in itself? The answer to this question cannot be settled in heaven, for it goes beyond direct divine control. Thus, in the end, God's opening challenge to the Satan is very risky, because it is interdependent on the motivation of Job on earth.

The counter-challenge by the Satan (2:4). The rhetoric of the accusation of the Satan is focused on Job, but the real thrust of it must ultimately be seen as being focused on God, for it is a response to the divine claim in vv. 1-3 about goodness and its effectiveness on humans. The counter-challenge, therefore, must be seen as a statement of doubt about divine power. The accusation of the Satan is carefully worded. He is not challenging the existence of God (obviously they are conversing), and the Accuser does not challenge God's concern and love for Job. Instead the Satan challenges the divine claim at the point where it becomes interdependent on Job. But even here the Satan is careful in his counter-challenge. His accusation is not theoretical about Job's ability to know or to communicate with God. Rather, he challenges the integrity of Job, by suggesting that Job fears God for profit—either to acquire wealth (the claim of the first cycle in 1:9-11) or to save his life (the claim of the second cycle in 2:4-5). It is important to see clearly the point of the counter-challenge. The Satan is suggesting that God's delight in the goodness of Job is actually manipulation by Job for his own profit. The issue of the Satan's challenge is neither sin nor its opposite, perfection (both of these could be, in fact, directly controlled by God). Rather it concerns the motivation of the godly person, which is, in fact, a statement of doubt about the power of the divine to influence humans at their most fundamental level.

The test (2:5-10). The Satan devises a test: "But stretch out your hand now and touch his bone and his flesh, and he will curse you to your face" (2:5). God agrees and the wording of the text is noteworthy, for the story moves beyond the direct influence of God, which it must do to satisfy the central point of the challenge: "Very well he is in your power" (v. 6a). In order to test whether or not Job's motivation is pure (i.e., an end in itself), his relationship with God must appear to be unprofitable and even hazardous. As the remainder of this section illustrates, Job stumbles but survives this initial blow.

The prologue to the book of Job is not primarily about Job. He emerges as a central character in the dialogues of chapters 3–37. The best way to preach the prologue of Job is to keep the focus on God and the Satan in heaven, and to raise the question: What does the Accuser doubt about God? A paradox then follows. The Accuser questions the effectiveness of God at its most vulnerable point, where divine power passes from actions (that could be directly controlled) to independent human motivation. Once framed this way, then God is the vulnerable character and not Job, because the truth of the opening divine claim (that there is such a thing as goodness in humans) rests on Job's response and not on anything that God does (hence the silence between God and Job for most of the book). Job can respond in three ways at this point. First, he could take his wife's advice by cursing God and dying. If he curses God because of the absence of good things in his life, then he would actually have been manipulating God for his own profit. His love for God would evaporate with the profit motive, and, certainly, the Satan would be correct because God would have been hoodwinked by Job. Second, Job could interpret the disasters as something he deserves (the point of view of his friends in the following chapters which will be the topic of interpretation next week). But this is no better than cursing God and dying, since an interpretation of disaster as justified punishment is simply another way for Job to concede that God had no lasting or transformative effect on him. Here the tables would be just the reverse, for if Job saw no permanent change arising from his allegiance with God, then he would have been hoodwinked by the divine. The third response is that Job hold fast to his integrity by holding on to God as an end in itself, which would then provide insight into his motivation. There is a twist here because, although the third option accentuates Job's independence, it, in fact, supports God's opening claim about divine power and its influence on humans. Thus, in the end, the divine claim about goodness in humans rests with Job and not God.

The Response: *Psalm 26*

A Lament

Setting. Psalm 26 is a lament by one who is falsely accused, and who has fled to the sanctuary for asylum.

Structure. The psalm separates into four parts. It begins with an appeal to God to act as judge for the innocent person (vv. 1-3). Second, there is an oath of cleansing and declaration of innocence (vv. 4-7). Third, vv. 8-10 are a call for help in the setting of the sanctuary. And, finally, there is a concluding appeal to God to act as judge for the innocent person (vv. 11-12).

Significance. When the psalm is read in conjunction with the prologue of Job, it switches the focus from God and the Satan in heaven to Job on earth, for the psalm is the voice of the innocent sufferer.

New Testament Texts

The lesson from Hebrews brings together passages that present high Christology and root it in the person and work of Jesus. The verses from Mark are a series of scenes recalling Jesus' teaching about divorce and inheriting the kingdom of God.

The Epistle: *Hebrews 1:1-4; 2:5-12*

But Now by God's Son

Setting. This lesson is the first in a series of eight readings from Hebrews. We encountered Hebrews during Lent and Holy Week of Year B. This discussion of setting repeats some of the information given at that time, and it will serve as a general introduction to the text from Hebrews for the subsequent weeks.

Commentators like to point out that Hebrews begins like a treatise, proceeds like a sermon, and ends like a letter; yet, the central sermonic materials that make up the bulk of the writing have an enigmatic philosophical cast unlike most Christian preaching today. The document is a grand meditation on the superior character of the new Christian covenant, designed to undermine any nostalgia for the previous covenant that could motivate a return to former things. In its development Hebrews makes an intimate connection between theological argument and the interpretation of scripture. In particular, this week's lesson comes from the introductory section of Hebrews (1:1–2:18). In this portion of the letter the author works with a collection of passages from the Old Testament about angels and argues the superiority of Christ over the angels.

Structure. The two sets of verses that compose our lesson come from three distinct steps in the author's exposition. The first four verses are the formal introduction to the work, and they resound with the major theological themes of the complete composition. In these lines we encounter several structural elements. There is a contrast between "long ago" and "these last days," between "the prophets" and "a Son," and between "the Son" and "angels." In the course of making these contrasts, the author gives information about who God's Son is and what the Son has done (and is doing).

The second set of verses falls into two parts. Hebrews 2:5-9 sharpens our focus on the Son, naming Jesus and referring to his vicarious suffering and death. Verses 10-12, in turn, are part of 2:10-13 (or 18). They refer to Jesus' suffering to emphasize his humanity, which makes him one with other humans in relation to God.

Significance. It is nearly impossible to exhaust the possibilities for proclamation in these verses. But whatever line one takes in relation to this lesson, the overarching concern of the author that must inform any sermon is the magnitude of God's saving work in his Son, Jesus Christ, which surpasses all else that has gone before (and by implication, anything that follows)

The text begins by framing its proclamation in terms of God's time. God has worked in the past in a variety of ways, and the author singles out the prophets for special mention—perhaps because of the relationship between their work and preaching and what the author contends God accomplished in Jesus Christ. Yet now God has gone beyond all that went before by speaking to humanity through his Son. We learn that this Son is "heir to all things"—that is, he has been named master of all God's creation—and that this is especially fitting because it is through this Son that God created all that God brought into existence. The beauty of this scheme is its sense of continuity and completion. The one through whom God gave creation its beginning is now established as the one to whom all creation belongs. Thus, the Son is both creator and Lord.

In turn, we learn more about (1) who the Son is, (2) what he has done and is doing, and (3) what that means. First, the Son is "the reflection of God's glory and the exact imprint of God's very being.'' Second, he has ''made purification for sins'' and he ''sustains all things by his powerful word'' as he sits ''at the right hand of the Majesty on high.'' Third, this means in his person and work he is ''much superior to angels.'' Seeing the point these lines make is helpful, but each of these phrases (and others in the text) are theologically loaded, and careful consultation of a serious scholarly commentary is practically required. In brief, however, these phrases articulate a high Christology that asserts the divinity, preexistence (incarnation, not explicit here), exaltation, and rule of the Son. The author believes the Son created, redeemed, and rules the world, which had its beginning and now is sustained by God's power at work through the Son.

Lest we float away in abstract glory, the second portion of our lesson imbues this Christology with the author's explicit, concrete, and historical vision. We focus on Jesus. The mention of this name puts flesh on the author's Christology. That Jesus ''for a little while was made lower than the angels'' makes explicit the author's earlier assumption about incarnation. In turn, the mention of Jesus' suffering gives a historical location to the previously mentioned ''purification for sins'' in the vicarious experience of Jesus, who as God's Son made God's grace effective by tasting death for everyone. Indeed, the humanity of Jesus brings God and humanity together in a redemptive bond that means salvation for humanity because of what God has done for humans in and through Jesus.

The Gospel: Mark 10:2-16

Divorcing and the Great Divorce

Setting. We continue to examine material in the collection of Jesus' teaching that follows the second prophecy of Jesus' Passion and the second misunderstanding of the meaning of discipleship among Jesus' closest followers.

Structure. The lesson has three parts. The first two are obviously related, but the third part seems simply to follow in the wake of the others. In vv. 2-9 we have the account of Jesus' sharp conversation with the Pharisees about divorce. Following this, in typical Markan fashion, we have the report of a private conversation between Jesus and the disciples concerning this same subject. With the disciples, as always in private, Jesus speaks bluntly and clearly (vv. 10-12). Finally, vv. 13-16 recount the reaction and teaching of Jesus when the disciples hindered children from approaching their master. Explicit or implicit in each of these sections is Jesus' viewing matters from God's point of view rather than from a simple human perspective.

Significance. Because the dramatic lesson in vv. 13-16 is close to that in the Gospel lesson for Proper 20, we shall give our attention to vv. 2-12.

Some Pharisees went to Jesus asking whether he thought it was lawful to divorce. Mark says they were testing Jesus. In the context of his entire Gospel, we know what he means. Mark 3 says the Pharisees and the Herodians (political supporters of Herod Antipas) were in league to destroy Jesus. Mark 6 recalls the clash between John the Baptist and Herod Antipas over Herod's marrying Herodias, and Herod killed John for criticizing them. Mark 10:1 says Jesus was in Peraea, Herod Antipas's political domain. Thus, the motive of this testing is clear. Pharisees ask Jesus about the legality of divorce and hope he will say something that will infuriate Herod, who will then surely kill Jesus, as he did John.

Jesus saw what the Pharisees were up to; and so, he didn't answer them. Rather, he asked them a question, "What did Moses command?" And quite easily the Pharisees quoted Deuteronomy 24, "Moses allows a man to write a bill of divorce and put his wife away."

Having heard the Pharisees, Jesus said (literally), "To the hardness of your heart Moses wrote you this commandment." In fact, there is nothing in Moses' law providing for divorce. Deuteronomy 24 refers to divorce, but it does not endorse it. It recognizes the reality of divorce, and it gives restrictions and limitations for the established practice—that is, when Deuteronomy was written husbands were already divorcing their wives. Deuteronomy 24 simply insists that a woman be given a bill of divorce to prove she was free, so that she could remarry and not be regarded or condemned as an adulteress.

Notice the word Jesus uses for "hardness of heart." It is related to the verb used in Exodus when God hardens Pharaoh's heart. Think about it. God hardened Pharaoh's heart; and so, Pharaoh was set against God's will. Thus, listen to Jesus as he speaks about hardhearted people. Hardhearted people (the ones divorcing in this case) are like Pharaoh, they are opposed to God's will.

Jesus rejects the compromised position of the Pharisees. He shows no interest in debating Deuteronomy 24. Instead, he takes Genesis 1 and 2 as his text. The Pharisees had the wrong text! They ask about divorce and quote a passage that tells them how to do it; but when Jesus speaks he recalls the creation stories. Jesus moves the conversation to a new plane by declaring the absolute will of God, expressed in God's purposeful creation. We and the Pharisees think and talk about ourselves, but Jesus talks about God. Thus, in vv. 10-12, Jesus speaks from an unearthly point of view. Our starting point is human, but Jesus' starting point is divine. We talk about divorce and divorcing; but Jesus sees clearly that the problem is the Great Divorce of ourselves from the will of God. We are divorced from God and all our divorcing is but sad evidence of it!

We need to see that Jesus' words do recognize a terrible fact: We humans can and do separate what God united. We can affect God's divine plan. We often do thwart God's will. We can and do fracture God's handiwork by divorcing and by living in the midst of the Great Divorce from God. And that's the bad news of this text. But there is good news: the gospel of Jesus Christ. God is with us in our marriages, and God in Christ is with us in our lives. The promise to faith is that the mercy of God provides the basis of both marrying and living. Our marriages and our lives are not ours alone. They are gifts from God, and, in the middle of marriage and life, God in Christ is with us!

Proper 22: The Celebration

For many congregations this set of lessons will occur on the Sunday observed as World Communion Sunday. At first glance they appear to offer little, if any, insight into the day's theme. What must be remembered, as was stated in the introduction to this volume, is that the observance of the Lord's Supper is not an end in itself, but is a way of reminding Christians just how intimately Christ is with them in all the moments of life.

The epistle lesson is the hermeneutical tool for interpreting the other lessons in relation to the World Communion emphasis. Here Christ is portrayed as the divine Son who has fully participated in our human existence and experienced the fullness of human suffering and brokenness. As God trusted Job (see exegesis), so God trusts Jesus to substantiate the divine claim about human goodness when we fail to do so, and in Jesus we are brought to glory. The brokenness of our lives is countered by the bread broken and shared around the table. The divorces of individuals and of the Christian churches are met by a call to be a new creation, and at the table we sample the appetizers of the banquet of the new age that Christ makes possible. It is World Communion Sunday because the host has tasted death for everyone (Hebrews 2:9).

Intercessions for today might include all innocent sufferers, those who wrestle to understand the will of God for their lives, divorced persons and those struggling to save their marriages, Christian unity, and children. Prayers may also be offered for those who grow wheat and bake bread, who grow grapes and make wine.

Liturgical planners may wish to incorporate acts of worship that represent the Church around the world. Hymns and prayers from different traditions may be employed. One or more lessons may be read in another language as well as English, particularly if there are native speakers of it in the congregation. The Lord's Prayer might also be used in another language. A large globe or map could be included in the day's visuals. "Lift High the Cross" will fit well as the day's opening or closing hymn.

Proper Twenty-three Sunday Between October 9 and 15 Inclusive

Old Testament Texts

Job 23:1-9, 16-17 is one of Job's concluding responses to his three friends, who have come to comfort him. Psalm 22 is a liturgy that includes a range of expression from lament to thanksgiving.

The Lesson: Job 23:1-9, 16-17

Doubts About Job

Setting. The tradition history of the book of Job is difficult to trace. The core of the book in chapters 3–27 consists of dialogues between Job and his three friends (Eliphaz, Bildad, and Zophar), who represent different voices within Israel's wisdom school. These dialogues appear to have been expanded by the additional speeches of Elihu in chapters 32–37, and, furthermore, all of the speeches are presently introduced by the prologue in Job 1–2. Whatever the exact traditional-historical development of the book of Job may have been, it is clear that the prologue is now meant to provide the hermeneutical key for reading the speeches. In the commentary on Job 1:1; 2:1-10 for Proper Twenty-two, we noted the careful division between God and minor deities in heaven versus Job and other humans on earth. There the focus seems to be on God in heaven and the accusation by the Satan concerning the divine claim about goodness in humans. That focus changes at the conclusion of the prologue from heaven to earth in 2:11-13, when three of Job's friends come to comfort him, at which time the heavenly scene is closed off. The fading away of the heavenly scene, however, must not prevent us from seeing the parallel between God and the sons of God (especially the Satan) in heaven and Job and his three friends on earth. The parallel suggests an interdependence between Job and God and the Satan and the three friends, even while it underscores both a change in focus from heaven to earth, and the silence between God and Job that provides the central tensions throughout the book. Given these parallels the friends are best interpreted as taking up the role of the Satan, but in relationship to Job rather than God.

Our central problem of interpretation, therefore, will be just the reverse of last week—namely, to determine what it is that the three friends doubt about Job. There is a twist, however, to the confrontation between Job and his three friends that was absent in the exchange between God and the Satan. As representatives of Wisdom the three friends mask their role as Accusers under a cloak of piety and orthodoxy, which means that integrity for Job will only be maintained at the cost of apparent heresy. Job will certainly need God to vindicate his position, since it will go against his own religious tradition.

Structure. The dialogues in chapters 3–27 separate into three cycles. The first cycle consists of chapters 3–14. This cycle begins with a speech by Job, which sets the mood of the dialogues (chapter 3), before each of the three friends and Job go through an exchange: Eliphaz and Job in chapters 4–7, Bildad and Job in 8–10, and Zophar and Job in 11–14. The second cycle consists of 15–21: Eliphaz and Job in 15–17, Bildad and Job in 18–19, Zophar and Job in 20–21. The lectionary text comes from the third cycle which consists of chapters 22–27. This cycle is abridged and consists of speeches by Eliphaz (chapter 22) and Bildad (chapter 25) with responses to each by Job (chapters 23–24, 26–27). Job 23 is Job's response to the accusations of Eliphaz in chapter 22 that Job deserves his present suffering.

Significance. The exchange between Job and his friends has been going for many chapters. In these chapters the focus of discourse has tended to be more abstract—about the nature of humanity in general and the relation between humans and the divine. The character of the discussion changes in chapter 22. This chapter provides a necessary prologue for preaching chapter 23, since the latter is Job's response to the arguments put forth in chapter 22.

Eliphaz has serious doubts about Job's claim to be an innocent sufferer, and, in chapter 22, he now bares down very directly to make his point. He accuses Job of being wicked (v. 5) and then provides evidence. Job is guilty of extortion from his own family (v. 6), he is oppressive and selfish—he takes away clothing from the poor, water from the weary, bread from the hungry, and ignores the widow and orphan (vv. 6-9). It is necessary to probe below the surface of these accusations in order to uncover a two-part theology that is providing the authority for the conclusions of Eliphaz. First, Eliphaz claims to have insight into divine motivation, which he expresses in vv. 2-3. He concludes that God is not motivated by righteousness in humans, because nothing about humans could ever be profitable for God. He states: "Can a mortal be of use to God? . . . Is it any pleasure to the Almighty if you are righteous or is it gain to him if you make your ways blameless?" This argument is meant to provide the basis for his second point stated in v. 10, which is the necessity for a strict theology of rewards and punishments, if humans are to have any insight into God. In view of these two presuppositions, Job must realize that he is evil and thus deserves his suffering.

Eliphaz has taken the place of the Satan. Note how his accusation against Job is also about motivation, but that its content is just the reverse of the Satan's claim against God in the prologue. The Satan questioned the divine claims that there was goodness in humans. He did this by questioning human motivation. The core of the Accuser's claim was that Job participated in salvation for profit. As we saw last week, once the issue is framed in this way, God is the vulnerable character, because only Job can verify the divine claim that there is goodness in humans. Eliphaz also questions the effect of divine goodness on humans, but his focus is on Job rather than God. Thus he questions Job's claim of goodness or integrity, not on the basis of Job's motivation but on the basis of divine motivation. The core of his claim is that human righteousness is not profitable for God, that it is not an end in itself for God. Therefore, the only way to trace divine motive is through a strict theology of rewards and punishments. Within this theological framework suffering is the most reliable indicator of divine motive for it signals divine involvement aimed at changing behavior. Eliphaz's solution, therefore, is simple: Job must give up his claim to innocence and interpret his suffering as deserved punishment, so that he can get on track with God. This is a powerful argument: It accentuates the absolute power of God; it advocates a piety about human evil and unworthiness before God, which gives the appearance of humility; and it addresses the problem of suffering. It is flawed because it lets God off the hook with the simple solution that good things come from God and evil things come from humans. But if this is true, then what is the point of making allegiance with God, because there is nothing permanent or transformative for humans in such actions? In other words, it is not possible to become a new person through the power of God. And this is why Job cannot agree with Eliphaz, but instead claims his innocence in the context of suffering. Job is saying at least three things: One, that divine goodness has lasting effects on humans. This conclusion leads to two others that are interdependent: God does, indeed, delight in human righteousness as an end in itself; and that suffering, therefore, cannot be a reliable indicator of divine motive.

The role of Eliphaz as a teacher of Wisdom requires further comment since he is presented as a representative of orthodoxy. This merging of orthodoxy and doubt about human goodness is a trap that is far more cunning than the Satan's accusation in the prologue. Much more dangerous is that Eliphaz claims to speak for God, which was never the case with the Accuser in the prologue, and, furthermore, Eliphaz's advice is presented as a clear statement of divine motive by one who should know about such things in a situation were experience certainly appears to support his argument. Job is presented with the unsavory choice of being religious and letting God off the hook, or of hanging on to God and being a heretic. The central point of tension in chapters 22–23 is this: The seemingly pious choice of interpreting disaster as justified punishment is, in fact, another way for Job to concede that God has had no lasting or transformative effect on him. Thus, God's opening claim about human goodness is just as much at stake in chapters 22–23 as it was in the prologue, and Eliphaz's piety is no less dangerous to both God and Job than the more direct advice of

Job's wife at the close of the prologue, when she encouraged him to curse God and die. Although the issue has remained the same through the book of Job (the possibility of goodness in humans) the challenge in chapters 22–23 is structured in just the opposite way from the prologue. Chapters 22–23 concern divine motive rather than human motive, and they raise the following question: Has God manipulated Job into thinking that righteousness is an end in itself, when in fact it is not? Just as the Satan's doubts about God could only be answered in the end by Job, since they concerned human motivation, so, too, must the doubts of orthodoxy about Job's innocence ultimately be answered by God, since they concern divine motivation.

The lectionary text is Job's response to Eliphaz. The power of this text is that it completely ignores the arguments of Eliphaz, which, quite frankly, are too strong given Job's present circumstances. Instead, Job addresses the silence between himself and God. The language takes on legal connotations. Job has a complaint against God (v. 2), and he wishes to lay his case before God (v. 4). The rebelliousness of Job's language appears blasphemous against the piety of Eliphaz. Yet it is the directness of Job's complaint against God for being absent that demonstrates his integrity and allows him to pass the test momentarily. But there is no closure to this text, because God never enters into the dialogue. We leave the text with the conflict between piety and integrity unresolved, and that is how this text should be preached. The power of this text is not in reaching a conclusion, but in preaching its central messages: (1) God needs humans and humans need God to achieve genuine goodness in this world (the prologue to the book of Job and chapter 23). (2) God does take pleasure in righteousness (contra Eliphaz in 22:2-3). (3) Permanent change takes place in the godly person with the result that life-experience cannot be a reliable indicator of character (contra Eliphaz in 22:4-11). And (4) Unjust suffering is not a sign of divine punishment, but of divine absence (23:1-9). A paradox emerges here, for by ignoring the arguments of Eliphaz and by maintaining his innocence through a complaint against God, Job actually keeps God in the situation of his suffering. If Job didn't do this the book would end at chapter 22.

The Response: *Psalm 22:1-15*

A Lament

Setting. This psalm is well known to Christians because it has been taken up into the Passion story of Jesus in the New Testament. The entire psalm includes a variety of forms from lament and prayer to praise, which suggests that Psalm 22 may have functioned as a liturgy. The lectionary reading is limited to aspects of the lament.

Structure. Psalm 22:1-15 separates into three parts. Verses 1-10 describe how the psalmist has been forsaken by God and by humans. Verse 11 is a cry for help, before the focus turns once again in vv. 12-15 to a description of how the psalmist is surrounded by enemies.

Significance. The psalm expands the language of Job's address to God in chapter 23. It, too, probes the problem of divine absence (v. 1) and the consequences this has on the psalmist who looks for some sign of God's presence. In such an extreme situation of suffering, the very language of either complaint or lament becomes the only cord connecting the sufferer and God.

New Testament Texts

The lesson from Hebrews offers profound christological teaching, which is applied to the conditions of human life as faced by believers. The verses from Mark combine conversations and teachings of Jesus to make a strong statement about the necessity of unswerving loyalty to God's call.

The Epistle: *Hebrews 4:12-16*

To Be Known and to Be Sustained by Jesus Christ

Setting. The first major section of Hebrews (after an extended introductory statement in chapters 1 and 2) begins in 3:1 and continues through 4:13. The author uses portions of Genesis 2, Numbers 14, and Psalm 95 to argue that the promises given to Israel are now open to Christians. After this, a second major section of the letter, 4:14–7:28, uses materials from Genesis 14 and Psalm 110 to antedate the cultic priesthood of Israel by referring to Melchizedek who functions in the author's argument as an ultimate priest-type for the greatest high priest of all, Jesus Christ. Remarkably, the verses of our lesson come from the ending of one section and the beginning of another.

Structure. The two distinct parts of the lesson, vv. 12-13 and vv. 14-16, each have dynamic internal logic. In the first segment we hear of the powerful, active, all-discerning Word of God; and we hear that the Word's judgment lays a final claim on our lives. Then, in the second segment we hear of Jesus, the Son of God, our high priest who passed through the heavens. We are reminded of his humanity and his capacity to sympathize with our human situation. Because of this Hebrews charges us to "hold fast to our confession" and to "approach the throne of grace with boldness" to "receive mercy and grace to help in time of need."

Significance. These striking verses are a grand christological lesson about the person, the power, and the purposes of Christ. The Christology, however, is far more than textbook teaching, for the author unpacks the Christology by applying it to the lives of believers. We learn that because of who Jesus Christ is and because of what he has done, is doing, and will do, a divine claim is laid on our lives, so that we are called to steadfastness and courage.

Verse 12 may be one of the most quoted, least understood, and most misapplied lines in the New Testament. Frequently defenders of the Bible cite this verse to support declarations about the authority of scripture, but if we read the text carefully we see that v. 12 begins a statement that is completed in v. 13. The Word of God in v. 12 is none other than Jesus Christ. It is he who is active, scrutinizing, capable of distinguishing at the most intimate levels of life, and genuinely discerning of the depths of our existence. This reference to Jesus as the Word of God recalls the declaration in 1:2, "in these last days [God] has spoken to us by a Son," and forms a powerful reminder to Christians that the heart of our faith and life is found in our God-given vital relationship to Jesus Christ. Thus, v. 13 does not so much turn in a new direction as it expands the mention of judgment in v. 12 by saying, "before him . . . the one to whom we must render an account." It is Jesus Christ ("heir of all things," 1:2) from whom nothing is hidden, and it is he whose work places an ultimate divine demand on our lives. The daring declarations of these verses are awe-inspiring, but as promise more than as threat.

The next verses advance the argument of the author by introducing fresh images and metaphors, but as we will see the author continues to address the same basic topic with which he has been engaged throughout the letter. The name of Jesus is introduced and qualified with titles such as "great high priest" (which itself is qualified with "who has passed through the heavens") and "Son of God." The profound respect of the author for the person of Jesus does not cause him to lose sight of Jesus' real humanity; indeed, the greatness of the heavenly high priest, the Son of God, is rooted in his being able "to sympathize with our weaknesses" because "in every respect [he] has been tested as we are, yet without sin." Jesus' real experience of the foibles of human life give him complete compassion for our limitations and difficulties, and his steadfastness despite temptation puts him in a position to give us exactly the help we need in life's exigencies. Thus, the author exhorts his audience to hold fast to their confession—that is, faith in Jesus Christ—and to approach the throne of grace. By approaching the throne of grace we come before the one who has the ability to keep us faithful amidst temptations. It is important to notice that Jesus Christ ministers to the needs of those who turn to him by "mercy and grace." We are not suddenly made sinless; rather, God's generosity and goodness underwrite our faithfulness.

For the writer of Hebrews Jesus is the object of Christian devotion, and he is the true source of faithful Christian life. Preaching on this lesson should tell the truth of Jesus Christ, call hearers to faithfulness, and illustrate the power and dependability of Christ to stand with us through temptation despite our weaknesses.

The Gospel: *Mark 10:17-31*

Discipleship and Eternal Life

Setting. These verses are the last pieces in the second cycle of prophecy, misunderstanding, and teaching in Mark 8–10. The teaching of Jesus in this section instructs disciples on a variety of topics, all of which address the true nature of discipleship.

Structure. The verses cohere in a developmental scheme, though we can view the stages of the text in isolation from one another without difficulty. Initially, we find a wealthy man approaching Jesus to ask about the requirements of inheriting eternal life. The conversation is exceptional, as are certain details of Mark's narration (vv. 17-22). After the departure of the man, Jesus addresses his disciples directly with stunning teaching about the liability of riches. The amazement of the disciples leads to a question, which draws a memorable pronouncement from Jesus (vv. 23-27). In turn, Peter makes a declaration about the loyalty of the disciples, and Jesus utters a final vivid saying.

Significance. We face another embarrassment of riches in this lesson. Both the contours and contents of the conversations and the small details of the narrative inspire reflection toward preaching.

The man comes to Jesus with a question that reveals his awareness that simply following rules, even the finest religious rules, is not finally sufficient for a real relationship with God. The man says he had kept the commandments, and there is nothing in the story to imply that he was deceiving himself or attempting to deceive others. Indeed, the opposite is the case, for Mark tells us that hearing of the man's devotion to the law, Jesus loved him. There is also nothing in Mark's manner of recounting this incident that implies Jesus' love was not real. And yet, the man seems to sense that there must be something more to life than keeping commandments. He asks about eternal life, and despite comments by interpreters to the contrary, his subsequent sad departure is no indication that his question was halfhearted.

We naturally expect to find the phrase *eternal life* in the Fourth Gospel, but we should be struck by the words and the idea in Mark where it is not a dominant theme. This commandment-keeper perceives that there is something more about a relationship with God, and it is so great that it transcends the boundaries of normal human existence. Moreover, whatever this form of relationship is, the man also knows that it comes from God, for he thinks and speaks of it as an inheritance.

Jesus is struck by the man's inquiry. At first it seems he puts the man off, however, by throwing the word *good* back at him. But recall that in earlier stories such at those of Jairus' daughter and the woman with the issue of blood (5:21-43) people perceived the presence of God in Jesus. Can it be that Jesus is probing the man's comprehension, attempting to see whether the man sees in Jesus' own person and work the real presence and power of God? Whatever this enigmatic exchange means, this line in the conversation ends, for the man makes no answer.

Instead, Jesus refers to the commandments, which it turns out the man has kept. Jesus' loving response to the man's devotion is to call him to discipleship. The origins of eternal life are rooted in discipleship to Jesus Christ. Thus, in this call Jesus offers the man the very thing he is hoping for, and now, not merely in the future. This call is not yet another commandment, not even the ultimate one; it is the offer of involvement that embodies in anticipation the reality which the man desires.

When the offer is made the man leaves in sorrow, for full involvement with Jesus calls him away from this world's priorities to those of God. In the ancient world (and ours!) people often took wealth as a sign of God's blessing, but the abundant life (another idea prominent in John, not Mark) offered by God through Jesus Christ is not defined by riches. This man lets the supposed symbols of God's approval take precedence over the reality of a relationship that is not symbolized or mediated through anything other than Jesus Christ.

Jesus tells his disciples of the peril of riches. Because they would assume wealth testified to divine blessing, they are astounded. They ask, "Then who can be saved?" But notice Jesus does not answer this question. The disciples cast the matter incorrectly. The real question is "Who can do the saving?" God and God alone, so that there is nothing we can or must do to inherit salvation; but to know the riches of a real relationship to God through Jesus Christ we must allow nothing to come between us and God in Christ. The more we have, the greater our peril.

The final exchange between Peter and Jesus takes this point even further. It is not the here-and-now that really matters, but "the age to come," which already in Jesus Christ is laying a claim on our lives and offering us the reality for which we otherwise find ourselves only hoping.

Proper 23: The Celebration

Part of the epistle lesson may be used either as the call to worship or the introduction to the confession of sin, as follows:

> Since we have a great high priest who has passed through the heavens, Jesus, the Son of God, let us approach the throne of grace with boldness, so that we may receive mercy and find grace to help in time of need. (Let us confess our sins before God and one another.)

If the call to worship is used, an appropriate opening hymn is "Hail, Thou Once Despised Jesus" (*AMEC Bicentennial Hymnal*, no. 175; Episcopal, *The Hymnal 1982*, no. 495; *The Presbyterian Hymnbook* (1955), no. 210; *Hymns for the Living Church*, no. 95; *The United Methodist Hymnal*, no. 325).

Today's Gospel lesson provides an opportunity to think positively about poverty in a culture that instinctively thinks of it as an evil upon which we wage war. It is important to distinguish between poverty, as the voluntary embrace of being satisfied with enough, and penury, which is destructive to human selfhood. One contemporary theologian has described apostolic poverty like this:

> Poverty . . . means the recognition that in the most real sense the world is mine, whoever owns it in the narrow technical sense. Poverty is thus the ability to enjoy the world to the full because I am not anxious about losing a bit of it or acquiring a bit of it. Poverty takes pleasure in a thing because it is, and not because it can be possessed. Poverty is thus able to taste the flavour of life to the full. (H. A. Williams, *Poverty, Chastity & Obedience: The True Virtues* [London: Mitchell Beazley, 1975], p. 40)

Listen, also, to St. John Chrysostom, at the end of the fourth century, describe the benefits of apostolic poverty:

> Poverty, to those who bear it wisely, is a great possession, a treasure that cannot be taken away; a staff most firm; a way of gain that cannot be thwarted; a lodging that is safe from snares. The poor man, it may be objected, is oppressed. But then the rich man is still more subject to adverse designs. The poor man is looked down upon and insulted. The rich man is, however, the subject of envy. The poor man is not so easily assailed as the rich man, offering, as the latter does on every side, countless handles to the devil, and to his secret foes; and being the servant of all, through the huge encumbrance of his affairs. Standing in need of many things, he is compelled to flatter many persons, and to minister to them with much servility. But the poor man, if he knows how

to act as one religiously wise, is not assailable even by the devil himself. Job therefore, strong as he was before this, when he lost all, became still more powerful, and bore away an illustrious victory from the devil! (*The Homilies of St. John Chrysostom, Archbishop of Constantinople, on The Statues, or To the People of Antioch* in A Library of Fathers of the Holy Catholic Church, [Oxford: John Henry Parker, 1847], pp. 50-51)

St. Francis of Assisi spoke of himself as being married to the Lady Poverty. In a prayer attributed to him, he bewails the world's rejection of positive poverty:

O my dear Lord Jesus, have pity upon me and upon my Lady Poverty, for I am consumed with love for her, and can know no rest without her. Thou knowest all this, my Lord. Thou who didst fill me with the love for her. But she sitteth in sadness, rejected of all; she, the Mistress of Nations is become a widow;—the Queen of all Virtues is become contemptible. (Joan Erikson, *Saint Francis and His Four Ladies* [New York: W. W. Norton, 1970], p. 82)

Proper Twenty-four
Sunday Between October
16 and 22 Inclusive

Old Testament Texts

Job 38 is a theophany of God from the whirlwind. Psalm 104 is a hymn celebrating the creative power of God.

The Lesson: *Job 38:1-7 (34-41)*

God Breaks the Silence

Setting. We have characterized the book of Job in the past two weeks as consisting of a narrative prologue in chapters 1–2, where the focus is primarily on God and minor deities in heaven, and of poetic dialogue in chapters 3–37, where the focus is on Job and his friends on earth. A common characteristic throughout both of these sections is the silence between heaven and earth, and thus between Job and God. Although the conversation in heaven was about Job, he was, nevertheless, excluded from the exchange. The tables are somewhat different on earth, for God is an active listener to the dialogues between Job and his friends. Yet, from Job's point of view, there is only divine silence. In the lectionary text for this week, God finally breaks the silence by appearing to Job in the whirlwind, and by raising a series of questions to him about creation and the way the world is structured. When viewed within the larger context of the book, the theophany must be seen as God's responses to the complaints that Job had leveled at God previously. The central aim in interpreting the theophany is to determine whether the appearance of God and the divine speech to Job adequately answer the problems represented in Job's innocent suffering.

Structure. The theophany of God to Job comprises most of chapters 38–41, and it can be separated into two distinct speeches, with separate responses by Job: the first divine speech includes 38:1–40:2 with a response by Job in 40:3-5, and the second divine speech comprises 40:6–41:34 with a response by Job in 42:1-6 (the lesson for next week). The boundaries of the lectionary text present some problems, because they include the opening (vv. 1-7) and closing (vv. 34-41) verses of chapter 38, which do not appear to correspond well with the subdivisions of the initial divine speech. The optional verses (vv. 34-41) do not form a coherent section. Note how the questions dealing with weather, cosmological forces, and constellations actually begin in v. 22, and how v. 39 changes the topic to nature, which continues through 39:30. Unless a lengthy reading is desired these verses are best excluded from the Old Testament lesson.

Problems also arise with vv. 1-7. The central problem is determining whether v. 7 ends a section as the lectionary suggests. If interrogatives are used as a guide, then v. 7 does not end a unit, because v. 8 lacks a specific interrogative. The next interrogative in Hebrew occurs in v. 12, which suggests that vv. 1-11 are a better unit for interpretation. Once the setting of theophany is established in v. 1, this unit is organized around two questions, which God places to Job: Who are you? (vv. 2-3) and Where were you when . . . ? (vv. 4-11). The second question provides the context for a review of God's creative power, which separates into two parts by content. Verses 4-7 have a joyous ring to them in talking about the creation of the earth, while vv. 8-11 have a more ominous ring in describing how creation also implied a restriction of the power of sea or chaos.

Significance. Job's friends have been relentless in providing specific reasons for his suffering, most of which had to do with human limitations and wickedness. Throughout this exchange Job has resisted his friends' reasoning. Now, finally, God enters the stage in chapter 38, and we expect specific answers to the problem of innocent suffering. Instead we get more questions from God. At the very least the divine speech is opaque, and it raises the question: Does God address anything of importance with regard to the innocent sufferer? Or is the theophany a form of divine filibuster—a blustery attempt to talk around the real issue through power language that is meant to overwhelm and, in the end, exhaust Job? Two issues must be addressed in interpreting chapter 38 with an aim to answer these questions: the first is the genre of the text as a theophany, and the second is the content of the divine discourse.

First, the genre of theophany. Two questions provide background for interpreting the form of chapter 38. First, what is it that Job has requested from God in the dialogues? Second, does the theophany in chapter 38 answer Job's request? The lesson from last week provides the starting point for determining what it is that Job has requested from God. In chapter 22 Eliphaz offered Job reasons to account for suffering by talking about God, while Job's response in chapter 23 was on another level altogether. He didn't want to talk about God, he wanted to see God: "Oh that I knew where I might find him, that I might come even to his dwelling!" (v. 3). Job's complaint is about divine silence, and whether that silence indicates complete indifference. Once Job has rejected Eliphaz's conclusions that he is the cause of his own suffering, the sustained silence nurtures the lingering question: Had Job been manipulated by God into thinking that he was genuinely good and thus a permanently important character in creation—when, in fact, God was off doing other things now? The sheer form of the theophany in chapter 38, apart from the content of the divine speech, is important in interpreting this chapter, for it is an answer to Job's request to see God. God is not indifferent to Job.

Second, the content of the divine speech underscores Job's important role in creation, and, in so doing, it places innocent suffering in a larger context. The divine questions—Who are you Job? and Where were you when I created the world?—have a rhetorical flavor to them. This means that the contrast between God and Job appears to be accentuated with the questions, which then implies answers from Job—I am nobody, and I wasn't there at creation. Clearly the rhetoric of the divine speech is meant to accentuate the otherness and creative power of God. But upon closer reading, we must also see that the questions are not simply rhetorical but real. The reason for this conclusion is that in earlier speeches Job has already listed most of the content of the divine speech. Note, for example, how Job tells Bildad in chapter 26 that God constructed the foundations of the earth (26:7 = 38:4-7) and in the process limited the power of the sea (26:8, 12 = 38:8-11). Central to theophany is revelation, but if we focus only on the content of the divine speech, God really isn't telling Job anything he doesn't already know. This situation would suggest that the divine questions to Job are to some extent real or literal. God genuinely wants to know who he is, and whether, in fact, he was at the creation. If we interpret the questions literally, then the theophany underscores the high regard that God has for Job in the larger context of creation, which is what started this whole story in the first place—God made a boast about the goodness of Job in the prologue (1:8; 2:3), which implied a certain degree of independence of motive in Job. Such independence opens the door for real questions about another, and that is what God is doing.

The content of the divine speech also addresses the problem of the innocent sufferer, but not in the direct and specific way that Job's friends sought to do. What does this mean? Job's friends sought to account for suffering by talking about God and by clarifying a singular divine motive in an ambiguous situation. Note how in the theophany God doesn't actually talk about God or divine motive. One suspects that if God did, God would become one of Job's friends by also attributing singular motive to situations that are inherently ambiguous. The test of the godly person is to trust divine motive and demand divine presence even when suffering is unjust. The theophany of God satisfies this demand, while the divine speech addresses the structural ambiguity of creation by describing its praiseworthy aspects associated with the earth (vv. 4-7) and its more sinister aspects of the sea, which are presently somewhat controlled but not absent (vv. 8-11). Given this ambiguous situation within the present structure of creation, the integrity or goodness of Job becomes all the more important. In the commentary two weeks ago, we noted how God and Job were interdependent in the book of Job. The literal questions that God places to Job in the lesson for this week underscore once again that Job is not a puppet of God, but has active influence in the creation. But how and when? The book of Job suggests that the integrity of the godly person—in a situation of innocent suffering—is one of the primary ways that humans aid God in controlling the chaos of creation.

The Response: *Psalm 104:1-9, 24, 35c*

Celebrating God's Creative Power

Setting. Psalm 104 is a hymn celebrating the creative power of God. As such it shows a connection to Genesis 1 in vv. 6 and 25 as well as to creation motifs from other cultures in the ancient Near East. Verses 19-24 have a marked resemblance to the Egyptian hymn of Akhenaton (*Amenophis IV*), especially with the encyclopedic listing of aspects of creation. In addition, references to primeval waters in vv. 6 and 26 also suggest the influence of Syro-Canaanite primeval flood mythology.

Structure. Psalm 104:1-9 separates into two parts. Verses 1-4 begin with a call to praise and then describe the creative power of God in a heavenly setting: God is clothed in light, he has made the heavens, rides the winds, and controls fire. Verses 5-9 shift the focus from heaven to earth to describe how the heavenly power of God has structured this world: God laid the foundations of earth and limited the power of the "deep." (This is the same word that is used to described chaos in Genesis 1:2.). Verses 24 and 35c conclude with language of praise.

Significance. This powerful psalm answers the question, Who are we in light of God's relationship to creation? The key for understanding who we are as the people of God rests in seeing how the psalm has taken the knowledge of God as creator and turned it into the language of praise by the worshiping congregation. Such a celebration of creation by the worshiping community provides definition of what it means to be human: To be human is to know God as creator and to know that creation is itself a gift of grace. We have not laid the foundations of the earth and we do not presently keep chaos at bay. Such knowledge can only prompt praise from us—which then, in turn, defines our character.

New Testament Texts

There is profound Christology in both of the New Testament texts for this Sunday, but the passages are quite distinct in form, style, and tone. Hebrews begins to explore the metaphor of high priesthood to communicate central Christian convictions about the person and work of Christ. Mark continues the pattern we have encountered during the past weeks, where Jesus' Passion predictions provoke misunderstandings among the disciples and require further teaching from Jesus.

The Epistle: *Hebrews 5:1-10*

The Source of Eternal Salvation to All Who Obey Him

Setting. We worked with the opening verses of the second major section of the letter, 4:14–7:28, last week. In this segment the author uses a variety of Old Testament materials to argue for the superiority of Jesus Christ over the Levitical priests. He does this by referring to Melchizedek who functions as an ultimate priest-type for Jesus Christ. Melchizedek antedates the cultic priesthood of Israel, and so he has historical precedence over the line of Aaron. Jesus Christ, as a high priest in the likeness of Melchizedek, thus establishes a better covenant. Our lesson speaks of what it means to be a high priest, how Christ came to be high priest, who he is, how he trained for this office, and what he accomplished.

Structure. The logic of this passage is chiastic. It begins with a two-part discussion of high priesthood, saying (A) a high priest is appointed on behalf of other humans with whom he shares human weakness and (B) he does not take this office on himself but is called by God. Next, the discussion focuses on Christ, saying (B´) he did not exalt himself but was appointed by God and (A´) as a human he became the source of salvation for others. Thus Christology is done using the metaphor of high priesthood to explicate the person and saving work of Christ.

Significance. This complicated argument interprets the significance of Jesus Christ using models from Israel's history and cultic worship and lines from Israel's literature. The author reasons in a sensible first-century Mediterranean fashion. Yet, the basic argument is typological and may stike us as peculiar. Consulting articles in a scholarly dictionary of the Bible on "typology" and "types" will aid comprehension greatly. In brief, this is a form of argument on the principle of analogy to a personal prototype—that is, some historical character or figure (here, high priest, Aaron, and Melchizedek) sets a pattern or establishes a standard that by comparison to a later person explains the significance of the later figure. In our lesson the basic typological argument is complicated by the introduction of quotations from the Old Testament in a prophecy-and-fulfillment scheme. Yet, even this element of the argument seems strange, for the texts from the Old Testament are not predictions that later came true; rather they are statements that had clear original literal meanings, but the lines now find fuller meanings as they are applied to a later situation or person (here, Jesus Christ).

The author establishes two basic points. First, a high priest is appointed on behalf of other humans. Because he shares the essential human condition with them, the high priest offers gifts and sacrifices for himself as well as for others. Thus, the work of the high priest brings mutual benefits to himself and others. Second, the high priest is not self-appointed but called out by God. Thus, the work of the high priest is divine in origin. Aaron was this kind of high priest.

Next, our lesson unpacks these basic matters in relation to Christ, but in reversed order. First, Christ did not exalt himself; he was appointed by God. To validate and amplify this point, the author quotes Psalms 2 and 110. In doing this he introduces the motifs of Sonship and Melchizedek. The matter of Christ's Sonship is not new, having been raised and examined from the outset of the letter through nearly every passage up to this point. Melchizedek here is a high priest, and that motif will be developed after the verses of our lesson. In our text for this week the lines from the Psalms simply work to verify God's appointment of Christ as high priest.

Second, in vv. 7-10 the author comes to the crucial issue in our lesson. The opening words, "in the days of his flesh," refer to Christ's humanity, the generic condition he shared with other human beings. We read how as a human Christ did, as high priests do, pray for himself. Yet, notice it is not for his sinfulness but for God to save him from death. Confronting death and turning to God for salvation, Christ learned perfecting obedience through his suffering. This is a hard notion to grasp, but essentially the author understands that Christ conquered human weakness by perfect devotion to God, despite the worst forms of adversity. Because Christ was the divinely appointed high priest and because he was human, his prayers and obedience are shared with other humans—specifically with "all who obey him." Christ became the source of eternal salvation, for as God saved him from death Christ's prayers and obedience were mutually applicable to others. Thus, God designated him a high priest on the order of Melchizedek.

The Gospel: *Mark 10:35-45*

Whoever Wishes to Be Great

Setting. With these verses we come into the third cycle of Passion-prophecy, misunderstanding on the part of the disciples, and subsequent teaching about discipleship. After Jesus' reference to his forthcoming suffering, death, and resurrection (10:32-34), our lesson recalls the misunderstanding of James and John and Jesus' teaching them and, then, the other disciples about how they are to live as his true followers.

Structure. The lesson begins with a conversation. James and John approach Jesus and make their request, but Jesus tells them they don't know what they are asking, they say they do, and Jesus concludes the conversation with a pronouncement (vv. 35-40). Verse 41 refocuses the narrative, reporting the indignation of the other disciples at what James and John did. In turn, Jesus calls all the disciples and explains how life among them is to be lived, ultimately qualifying his teaching by comparison with his own person and work (vv. 42-45).

Significance. Three times in Mark's account Jesus speaks of his Passion. We have seen Peter misunderstand; all the disciples miss Jesus' point; and now, James and John demonstrate their failure to grasp what Jesus had taught. The ploy of the sons of Zebedee, however, is intriguing. Peter was direct with his reprimand, the disciples were open in their discussion with one another, but now James and John come to Jesus independent of the others and ask him for an unspecified favor. "Will you do me a favor?" We have all been asked, and surely we have all been tempted to reply, "It depends on what it is"; and so, Jesus asks, "What do you want?" In a strange way the disciples are like us all, prone to sneaking around and apt to seek special privileges from God.

But, as we learn in this story, the sons of Zebedee miscomprehended Jesus so badly that they asked for something they certainly didn't intend—not understanding Jesus, they did not know what they were requesting. Real danger portends when we look at Jesus' power and we look away from his cross and, then, we hustle up to him with a self-serving request. As Jesus interacts with James and John we find that everything is qualified in terms of the cross. The references to cup and baptism are metaphors for the cross. The true test of discipleship is found in the challenge to follow our Lord in his selfless suffering on behalf of others. Jesus does not look beyond the cross to his resurrection and exaltation into glory; rather he looks squarely at the cross and finds the real purpose of his own person and work as well as the essential meaning of what it requires to be one of his disciples. In Jesus' reply we see that the cross is the ultimate criterion whereby we measure the authenticity of every dimension of our discipleship. The only promise Jesus makes to the sons of Zebedee is that they will drink his cup and be baptized with his baptism, but whatever else they get as his disciples is finally the business of God and is not a matter for bargaining. In this exchange we hear the rough word of the gospel calling us beyond ourselves at all costs. The call to discipleship is not a call to get a leg up on everyone else. We are called to follow Christ in the way of the cross.

In Jesus' words to the assembled disciples we hear once again his call in God's behalf for the reversal of this world's standards. Greatness, from God's point of view, is found in godlike graciousness, generosity, and service, not in achieving positions of privilege and power that win the accolades of human culture. And how slow we disciples have been in hearing Jesus' words. In the Church we follow the lead of our world and honor those who achieve greatness in the eyes of human institutions. We seldom show Jesus' courage in assessing life purely from God's point of view. We may serve God, but a life of service in this world still means recognition—plaques, citations, awards, memorials—for we are indeed like James and John. Even those who seek no reward for their faithful service have tokens of esteem thrust upon them because, like James and John operating on the sly, we cannot believe that every other disciple is not as essentially self-centered as we are. Yet Jesus' final words state the real standard of godliness and discipleship. Jesus came to serve, to give his life for the liberation of others. He sought and received no service. And for his work the only plaque he ever received was the one hung on his cross.

Proper 24: The Celebration

Today's lessons lead us to a consideration of the meaning of priesthood—the priesthood of Christ and the priesthood of all believers as we exercise it liturgically and in our daily living. It may be that the character of a congregation's liturgical life will change dramatically to the degree that the members identify themselves as priests in the event, but it is first necessary to understand what a priest is. Put simply, a priest is one who offers sacrifice to God. This is a revolutionary idea to those who think of going to church as an act of receiving, of what one "gets out of it," rather than what one puts into it. Consider how frequently new people in a community go shopping for churches on the basis of what the churches have to offer them (nursery, sports teams) rather than what they have to offer the churches. We may legitimately call into question the theological foundation of any church growth movement that is based on viewing persons as consumers rather than offerers.

Today's lessons relate priesthood to the offering of suffering. Jesus, even, "learned obedience through what he suffered." Since it did not come automatically to the human Son of God, much less can we expect it to come easily! Jesus offers up his suffering for the redemption of humankind, and it is this offering in which we participate in the eucharistic sacrifice. One section of the Great Thanksgiving is technically called the "oblation," the offering, and it is usually framed in language like this: "we offer ourselves in praise and thanksgiving as a holy and living sacrifice, in union with Christ's offering for us." This offering should be no dreamy and abstract thing. It needs to be incarnated in daily work, so that liturgy, the work of the people, is translated into the offering of daily work and suffering for the redemption of the world because we offer it "in union with Christ's offering for us." That is what James and John needed to learn in today's Gospel lesson. When Jesus asks

101

them if they can drink the same cup and undergo the same baptism as he, he is referring to his suffering. How poignant, then, that those who respond "We are able" are described later in the report, "All of them deserted him and fled" (Mark 14:50). The laity bring to the liturgy all their diverse experiences of life that have never happened before and in the common prayer offer them to God to be used in the sacrificial spirit of Jesus. With Job, the offering of their suffering "is one of the primary ways that humans aid God in controlling the chaos of creation" (see exegesis above).

The use of the hymn, "Are Ye Able," is questionable in relation to this text from Mark, since it seems not to appreciate the irony of the disciples' reply to Jesus. "Take My Life and Let It Be" is a more suitable choice.

Proper Twenty-five
Sunday Between October
23 and 29 Inclusive

Old Testament Texts

Job 42:1-6 is Job's final response to God at the close of the book.
Psalm 34 is a hymn of thanksgiving.

The Lesson: *Job 42:1-6, 10-17*

From Silence to Sight

Setting The title for this commentary is a mixed metaphor that
states the problem which has been running throughout the book of Job.
Divine silence in the midst of suffering has generated an enormous
quantity of speech about God—especially by Job's friends, even
though what Job wanted was to see God. The last words of Job in
42:4-5 refer to this mixed metaphor, when he states that he has been
hearing a great deal of talk about God lately, but now with the
theophany he has seen God. Sight leads to confession and repentance,
and, for all practical purposes, this action ends the book, even though
there is also a narrative epilogue. The final speech of Job raises the
question, What has the sight of God done for Job that allows the story
to end? Two general interpretations are traditionally offered at this
point. Both accentuate some form of conflict between God and Job.
One interpretation underscores the power of God over against Job, by
emphasizing the closing motif of Job's humbling. This humbling can
be interpreted either as a complete surrender of will by Job to God or

as a form of reconciliation between Job and God in that Job comes to a new knowledge of God, which makes it clear to him that God is in control of creation. In either case Job is put in his proper place over against a sovereign God. Another interpretation seeks to maintain Job's independence over against God by interpreting his words either ironically or as defiant speech. Both lines of interpretation raise problems for the central thesis that we have been establishing, which is that God needs Job and Job needs God to confirm the divine claim of integrity in Job, which the Satan has doubted from the outset.

Structure. Job 42:1-6 separates into three parts. Verses 1-2 are either a concession or a confession about divine power, which is followed by two sections (v. 3 and vv. 4-6). Each of these sections begins by quoting an earlier speech of God during the theophany, and then each ends with a response by Job. Job 42:1-6 should be the focus for preaching the Old Testament lesson. If the epilogue in vv. 10-17 is also read, then vv. 7-9 should be included, since the epilogue is meant to provide contrast between Job and his friends, which is lost with the present boundaries of the lectionary text.

Significance. Interpretation will focus on Job's final speech, which must be seen in the larger context of the book. A brief review of the thematic development of the book will set the stage for reading 42:1-6. The interpretation of the prologue (chapters 1–2) underscored how God needs Job to confirm the divine claim of goodness in humans, since the claim is ultimately about human motivation rather than human action. Job's response to his wife at the close of the prologue confirms the divine claim that Job loves God as an end in itself. The issue continues, however, in a new setting by shifting the confrontation from God and the Satan in heaven to Job and his friends on earth for the dialogues (chapters 3–37). There is tension between Job and his friends throughout these dialogues because Job's friends believe they have insight into divine motivation, which can adequately explain Job's suffering. Their confident conclusion is that God punishes evil, which means that suffering is a reliable indicator of human sin. Job, therefore, must simply repent of his wickedness. Job, on the other hand, has claimed innocence, which he can only maintain by claiming no insight into divine motivation. Job's resistance to accept a too easy solution about divine motivation is both his salvation and God's vindication of integrity in humans. But there is no resolution to the problem of human suffering in Job's resistance. He needs God, rather than theological discourse or the rejection of it, to confirm his innocence in the midst of suffering. Consequently Job complains repeatedly about divine absence, while he also reflects on the nature of divine power, which when viewed from a distance terrifies him.

Theophany in chapters 38–41 is a turning point in the book, because God responds to Job's complaint and breaks the silence. Once the situation is personal (Job and God in dialogue rather than Job and his friends talking about a silent God in an ambiguous situation), then Job's resistance to make any claims about divine motivation becomes questionable rather than a sign of his integrity. Thus, even though his initial response to God in 40:3-5 is masked with the rhetoric of piety, it is, nevertheless, a retreat into silence, which makes him a less vulnerable character than God, who, in the prologue (1:8; 2:3), took enormous risk in making strong claims about Job's motivation. Thus the story is out of balance at this point and it cannot yet end.

Job retreats from his pious silence in 42:1-6, with a speech that is dominated by motifs of knowledge. The Hebrew word for knowledge occurs four times (as a verb, *yada'*, vv. 2, 3, 4; and as a noun, *da'at*, v. 3), in conjunction with the verb meaning understanding (*bin*, v. 3) and the noun meaning counsel (*'esah*, v. 3). These motifs allow us to ask what it is that Job has learned about God. The key to interpreting this text lies in Job's opening words in 42:2. The NRSV translates this verse in the first person so that Job is presented as making a concluding statement about himself ("I know that you can do all things."). This translation, however, is not so clear, because the verb in this instance is *qere-kethib*. The consonants of the verb "to know" are written in Hebrew as a second-person masculine singular: "You know" (hence the Hebrew word *kethib* meaning "written"), but the Masoretes have written in vowels which encourage a first-person singular reading: "I know" (hence the Hebrew word *qere* meaning "say"). The NRSV has followed the Masoretic vowel pointing (the *qere*), even though such a reading would require another consonant than what is in fact written in the text. The stronger reading, both textually and theologically, is the second person, which would mean that Job's final statement begins with a declaration about God, rather than himself: "You know that you can do all things." When the verse is read in the second person, Job must be seen not only as leaving the security of silence, but also as leaving the safety of making "I" statements (e.g., "I see that you are powerful") in order to make a far more risky declaration about divine motive (e.g., "You know you are powerful"). In the end only God could confirm or unconfirm this statement for Job, which brings the story full circle. By leaving his self-imposed silence in 40:2-3, and by making a claim about divine motivation, Job finally makes himself equally vulnerable to God, who began this story with a somewhat similar declaration about Job's motivation. In this repetition the story reaches closure, because both God and Job have now acknowledged their dependence on each other to achieve integrity on earth.

But what is it Job has learned that has freed him to take such a risky step? He tells us in the remainder of his speech by quoting the important aspects of the preceding divine speech to him. He does not quote the power imagery of God to control creation and even the sea. As we saw last week, he knew that information already. Instead, he quotes the questions that God put to him: "Who is this?" (40:3 = 38:2) and "I will question you" (40:4 = 38:3 and 40:7). The real insight into God for Job is himself. He did not know that God was able to create a creature who could function as a distinct other from God, who could then even become the object of real questioning by God, and in the end be a necessary ally to confirm God's claim that integrity was possible in humans. For all of his allegiance to God throughout the dialogues, Job did not know this limitation of God with regard to persons of integrity, hence the questions were a surprise and a new insight into divine power. The second-person reference to God in v. 2 must once again be underscored at this point. With the confession, "You know your own power," Job makes no claims to describe the details of how such power is exercised, which was the major preoccupation of his friends. Instead, Job trusts this process to God, which paradoxically confirms the effectiveness of divine goodness on humans.

The Response: *Psalm 34:1-8 (19-22)*

Thanksgiving

Setting. The psalms that have been associated with the Joban texts over the past four weeks have primarily been laments. Psalm 34:1-8 shifts the focus of the response to thanksgiving, before shifting to wisdom speech in vv. 19-22. Psalm 34 is an acrostic psalm with two lines attributed to every Hebrew letter.

Structure. The acrostic requirements often overshadow other structures within a psalm, and this is also somewhat true of Psalm 34. Verses 1-8 could possibly be expanded to include vv. 9-10. The reason for this is that vv. 11-22 clearly shift the focus from praise and thanksgiving to the more didactic style of wisdom teaching. The first half of the psalm separates between vv. 3 and 4, with vv. 1-3 functioning as an introduction and vv. 4-8 (9-10) providing an account of how God has been gracious and hence worthy of praise.

Significance. As noted above, the psalm provides a fitting conclusion to the study of Job. Verse 4 is especially noteworthy when the psalm is read in conjunction with Job, since the thanksgiving of the psalmist is rooted in God's presence, which leads to several conclusions that the psalmist wishes to share about God's relationship to the one in need: God hears the cry of the oppressed (v. 6), protects (v. 7), answers (v. 4), and ultimately will rescue those who fear him (v. 7). This insight into God provides the basis for two conclusions: One, God is good (this is the reverse of God's statement about Job); and, two, those taking refuge in God's goodness are happy (Hebrew, *'asry*). Happiness includes actions that result from receiving divine blessing and rescue. These actions are not spelled out in the first half of Psalm 34, but simply characterized as "fear of God." The teaching in the second half of the psalm, however, does begin to draw out more concretely what kinds of action happiness entails.

New Testament Texts

As the lessons from Hebrews and Mark continue, we find the epistle still meditating on Jesus Christ as the ultimate high priest who has the permanent capacity to save all those in whose behalf he serves. Mark's text recounts a highly dramatic healing of a blind man, Bartimaeus by name; and in this healing we see the true life-style and path of Christian discipleship.

The Epistle: *Hebrews 7:23-28*

Celebrating Christ's Capacity to Save

Setting. As we have seen during the past two weeks, the second major section of Hebrews, 4:14–7:28, uses materials from Genesis 14 and Psalm 110 to antedate the cultic priesthood of Israel by referring to Melchizedek, who functions in the author's argument as an ultimate priest-type for the greatest high priest of all, Jesus Christ. Our lesson comes from the closing lines in this second section.

Structure. There are two basic parts to this lesson, each composed of three verses. The first section contrasts the many former high priests with Jesus who is the one high priest forever. The second section makes declarations about Jesus as the sinless and exalted high priest, explaining his superiority and contrasting the previous high priests, who were appointed by the law, with Jesus, who was appointed by the "word of oath." The argument of these two portions of the lesson are highly related. Together they make strong confessional statements about the superiority and complete sufficiency of Jesus as the permanent high priest who mediates and makes intercession in behalf of all who approach God through him.

Significance. The lines of our lesson are densely packed confessional materials, which in the context of Hebrews make a strong statement that has a polemical as well as didactic purpose. Careful study of Hebrews shows that the author is writing to Hebrew Christians—that is, former Jews or at least people of Jewish heritage who are now Christians. These Hebrew Christians are facing difficulties, and as they ponder their faith in Christ they seem to recall their heritage with nostalgia that may cause them to retreat from their confession of Christ to their traditional Jewish religion. In large part, this letter to these Hebrews seems designed to diminish wistful remembrances of pre-Christian religious life by depreciating the inherent value of the institutions and offices of Judaism through comparison with Christ and Christian faith. The author of Hebrews is not interested in pluralism, syncretism, or a compromise that will in any way lessen the uniqueness and supremacy of Christ and a life of faith in relation to him. For the author, in the mix of religions, Christianity stands above all others because of the person and work of the central figure in relation to whom the whole religion is formed. Nevertheless, the author is not extremely belligerent toward Judaism, rather he is adamant about Christ; his observations about the inferiority of Judaism are all formed out of his unswerving conviction of the superiority of Christ and the life of faith that is lived by believers in relation to him.

In our late twentieth-century world it is easy to view Hebrews as religious jingoism, primarily because we do not live in an era when Christianity is in the process of defining itself in relation to the Judaism out of which it arose. The question, What difference does Jesus Christ make? actually means something different for us from what it meant for the author of Hebrews precisely because of the very different life circumstances we are facing. For the author of Hebrews, to say an affirming word about Judaism would have been to deny what God accomplished in Jesus Christ; it would have been an encouragement to others to turn away from Christ. Thus, in this passage and throughout the epistle, the author forms contrasts that are meant to establish the veracity of Christian faith by illustrating its genuine superiority.

If we move away from the polemical interests of the author, his message can be viewed purely positively as a celebration of the wonderful blessing of Christian faith. Translated into positive terms for the context we live in today, the author says this: Because of what God has done and is doing through Jesus Christ, we who are members of the Christian community of faith have a religious experience in relation to God that is unified, permanent, saving, gracious, and above mere human mediation. God takes access to humanity through the Son, and through the same Son, those who believe in him have access to God. The relationship to God established by Jesus in behalf of believers is, therefore, above all, personal. Moreover, the person of the Son, as the perfect and permanent source of salvation who mediates between God and humanity, sets the character of our religious experience (perfect and permanent). The character of the Son, Jesus Christ, is the character of our confession and our relationship with God. And, on this new covenant God has spoken an affirming word ("word of oath"—see 7:2-22 citing Psalm 110:4) that assures us of the complete sufficiency of our faith tradition.

The Gospel: *Mark 10:46-52*

Learning to See That We May Follow

Setting. Readers are asked to consult the lengthy discussion of setting for the Gospel lesson for Proper Nineteen. As will be clear from that discussion, our lesson this week is the final segment of the crucial central portion of Mark's Gospel (8:22–10:52), with its focus on the true nature of discipleship. Geographically the story is set at Jericho with Jesus on his way to Jerusalem where he will experience his thrice-predicted Passion. Marking the march of Jesus toward Jerusalem gives the story a sense of urgency.

Structure. The lesson has the vague form of an ancient miracle account with problem, action in relation to problem toward solution, resolution with confirmation; but there are many twists, turns, and details in this story that indicate the basic idea of miracle is present only in the background of this story. The narrative has a cast of characters, named and unnamed, and a swirl of activity. It is, however, framed by references to "the way" in vv. 46 and 52 (in Greek the words for "roadside" and "way" are the same word), and there is a noticeable contrast between Jesus and the many at the beginning and Jesus and Bartimaeus at the end, which creates dramatic focus. In the course of the account, the lines spoken by the various characters are worthy of examination. Indeed, the structure and elements of this story are suggestive for preaching.

Significance. If this story is symbolic or paradigmatic as many interpreters suggest (see the discussion of setting for Proper Nineteen)—it is hard to read Mark's account in Greek and conclude otherwise—then, we should examine it carefully. Unfortunately, both the RSV and the NRSV obscure many of the story's most telling items through imprecise translation, so the following comments will attempt to walk through the details of the story to inspire further reflection.

We should see that Mark presents Jesus here at the height of his popularity with his disciples (likely more than the twelve, notice

Mark's manner of referring to "the twelve" and to "the disciples" who are a seemingly larger group) and a great throng following him. Throughout the previous passages, however, we have seen that even Jesus' closest followers have not fully comprehended who he is and what it means to answer his call to discipleship. Yet they all accompany Jesus who is headed for Jerusalem, though he is the only one who sees his true destiny.

Leaving Jericho Jesus passes a man who is reduced by disability to begging. His name was Bartimaeus, which means "son of Timaeus," and curiously Mark informs us that Bartimaeus was the son of Timaeus. Why underscore this name when most persons healed in Gospel miracle accounts are never named? Many ask, but no one has a fully gratifying answer. Perhaps the name and the reference to the man's parentage are meant to contrast with the shout, "Jesus, Son of David" to indicate that how one is understood is the result of to whom one is related. Bartimaeus salutes Jesus as the "Son of David," a title for the Messiah with pronounced national and political tones.

Despite his flattering rhetoric, the people rebuke Bartimaeus. The action shows the strong disapproval of the crowd, for the verb *rebuke* is used in Mark for what Jesus did to demons, what Peter did to Jesus, and what Jesus did to Peter. Yet, Jesus stops and tells the people to call Bartimaeus. Jesus' indirect summons becomes direct as the people tell Bartimaeus (literally), "Take heart, arise, he calls you." The people who would likely agree with Bartimaeus's assessment of Jesus nevertheless attempt to stifle him—a blind beggar was regarded as a worthless sort; yet, Jesus who regularly has commanded exorcised demons, enthusiastic disciples, and the exonerated disabled to silence hears the cry and calls the man forward in spite of his garbled perception.

Jesus asks (literally), "What do you wish I will do to you?" Bartimaeus replies (literally), "My Teacher, in order that I may see!" The new title for Jesus and the request itself show Bartimaeus's willingness to learn from Jesus, perhaps even his willingness to learn to see. Repeatedly Jesus sought to teach the disciples about his saving Passion, death, and resurrection; but repeatedly they demonstrated that they had not learned his lesson, that they could not see. Jesus says Bartimaeus's faith "saved him"—that is, made him truly whole, as God intended for him to be.

Bartimaeus is quite a contrast to the disciples. "Immediately," as the first disciples answered Jesus' call, Bartimaeus saw clearly and "followed [Jesus] in the way." Once blind, sitting by the way, Bartimaeus called to Jesus in his misunderstanding; but as Jesus called him, and he left his all behind to be healed and to learn from Jesus, Bartimaeus moved into the path of discipleship as he followed Jesus in the way, Jesus' way, forward toward the cross.

Proper 25: The Celebration

The reference to Job's ability to see God and the opening of the eyes of Bartimaeus in today's lessons suggests the use of liturgical materials that refer to light and sight. A fitting opening hymn is "Christ, Whose Glory Fills the Skies" (Episcopal: *The Hymnal 1982*, nos. 6, 7; *Hymns for the Family of God*, no. 293; *The Lutheran Book of Worship*, no. 265; *The Presbyterian Hymnal*, nos. 462-3; *The United Methodist Hymnal*, no. 173). Specific reference to Bartimaeus is made in "When Jesus the Healer Passed Through Galilee" (*The United Methodist Hymnal*, no. 263). This would serve well as a Junior Choir response to the Gospel reading. For a sung prayer for illumination before the reading of the lessons or the sermon, use "Open My Eyes, That I May See" (*AMEC Bicentennial Hymnal*, no. 285; *The Baptist Hymnal*, 1991, no. 502; *Hymns for the Family of God*, no. 486; *Hymns for the Living Church*, no. 350; *The Presbyterian Hymnal*, no. 324; *The United Methodist Hymnal*, no. 454).

The following suggested opening prayer draws together themes from all three of today's lessons.

> O God, light to the blind and joy to the troubled,
> in your only-begotten Son
> you have given us a high priest, just and compassionate
> toward those who groan in oppression and sorrow.
> Listen to our cry;
> grant that all may recognize in him
> the tenderness of your love,
> and walk in the way that leads towards you.
> We ask this through our Lord Jesus Christ, your Son,
> who lives and reigns with you
> in the unity of the Holy Spirit,
> one God, for ever and ever.
>
> (G. Thomas Ryan, *Sourcebook for Sundays and Seasons: 1991—Year B*
> [Chicago: Liturgical Training Publications, 1990], p. 204)

The lesson from Hebrews suggests the use of one of Charles Wesley's greatest hymns, "Arise, My Soul, Arise." It is omitted from United Methodism's most recent hymnal (its first omission from an American Methodist hymnal), probably because of its implied Anselmian doctrine of atonement. Its real importance, however, is its vision of Christ as priestly intercessor. The hymn may still be found in the United Methodist 1964 *The Book of Hymns* (no. 122), as well as the *AMEC Bicentennial Hymnal* (no. 269), *The Mennonite Hymnal* (no. 244), and *Hymns for the Living Church* (no. 250), where a verse from today's epistle lesson is cited along with the hymn.

Preachers should note that in the commentaries on Job and Mark mention was made of the importance of working with translations that help the reader get as close to the original text as possible. Indeed, in today's case, the translations may prevent the preacher from getting significant insights for preaching! This might provide an opportunity in preaching to remind congregations that every translation is to some degree an interpretation and so begin to involve them with the preacher in deeper examinations of the text. To help lay persons engage in genuine exegetical study and to provide them with the tools for doing so is nothing less than an act of liberation that can open their eyes and help them follow Jesus more responsibly in the way.

Proper Twenty-six
Sunday Between October 30 and November 5 Inclusive

Old Testament Texts

Ruth 1:1-18 introduces the characters and events that make up the story of Ruth. Psalm 146 is a hymn of praise.

The Lesson: *Ruth 1:1-18*

Rumors of Life in the Midst of Death

Setting. The opening verse of the book of Ruth establishes both the time of the story line and the occasion: "In the days when the judges ruled, there was famine in the land." This temporal reference has influenced the placement of the book in the Protestant and Catholic Bibles between Judges and I and II Samuel. In this location the historical setting of the story is emphasized with the result that the book of Ruth is read as a link between the period of the judges and the monarchy. This relationship is underscored by the genealogy at the close of the book, which traces the offspring of Boaz and Ruth through King David. When the book is read as a hinge, its internal contrast between famine and death in Elimelech's family at the beginning of the story as compared to the abundant harvest along with the promise of new life in the marriage of Boaz and Ruth at the end of the story provides a springboard for interpretation on a larger scale between the end of the period of judges and the beginning of the monarchy period.

In the Hebrew Bible, however, Ruth is contained in the third section of Scripture—the Writings, where it is part of the five Festal Scrolls (Ruth, Song of Songs, Ecclesiastes, Lamentations, and Esther). The title Festal Scrolls arises because each of these five books is read with different festivals. The book of Ruth is read with the Feast of Weeks (Hebrew, *shavuot,* meaning "a unit of seven" or "a week"). The Feast of Weeks occurred on the day following the seven weeks after Passover (7 weeks = 49 days + 1 = 50 days), so that it is also called Pentecost (the Greek word meaning "fiftieth day"), although the latter term is more common in the Christian tradition, where the fifty days are numbered from Easter rather than Passover. The Feast of Weeks can also be called the Festival of First Fruits, because it celebrated the Spring barley harvest. The Festival of Weeks (*Shavuot*) or First Fruits was how ancient Israel acknowledged God's ownership of the land and gift of food each year. Thus there is a creation aspect to the festival, which celebrates how God is the giver of life through the produce of the earth. One reason why the book of Ruth is associated with the Feast of Weeks is because the barley harvest provides an important setting for the story. As Israel's worship traditions developed, however, the Feast of Weeks became historicized in Judaism with the giving of the law on Mount Sinai. In this interpretative context, the people of Israel actually become the first fruits of God by entering into covenant with him during the fiery revelation of the law on the mountain. The book of Ruth is also important for the celebration of the law and the birth of Israel, since the central character, Ruth, embodies the process of entering into covenant with God and the people of God.

Structure. The opening reference to Bethlehem in 1:1 as the home of Elimelech and the concluding genealogy of David in 4:13-22 holds firmly the Davidic monarchy as a backdrop to the story. The notice of a famine in Bethlehem in 1:1 over against the glimpse of the future outcome of the offspring of Boaz and Ruth provides the point of tension that moves the plot of the story along from death to the hope of life. The four chapters in the book of Ruth provide roughly four scenes in the progression of the story. Chapter 1 begins with death and famine. The movement of the story is away from the promised land to Moab in a quest for life, which, in fact, only leads to more death. This

115

chapter ends with Ruth and Naomi returning to Judah. Chapters 2 and 3 describe how Ruth and Naomi seek to establish a life in Judah, these chapters also introduce the character of Boaz and begin to develop both the legal and emotional relationship between him and Ruth. Chapter 4 brings the story full circle with Boaz formalizing a marriage to Ruth through legal action at the city gate (i.e., the equivalent of the law court in ancient Israel).

The lectionary text includes 1:1-18. This unit ends with Ruth's confession that she would follow Naomi at any cost. This confession is central to the story, but it does not include the closing words of Naomi in vv. 19-22, in which she describes her situation as being empty by renaming herself Marah (bitter) rather than Naomi (pleasant). The preacher may wish to add these verses if the emphasis on death and famine will be stressed in the sermon.

Significance. This story is not primarily about Elimelech, Naomi, or Boaz. It is a story about the Moabite woman, Ruth. Interpretation, therefore, must remain firmly focused on her, and other characters must be interpreted in relation to her. With this principle of interpretation as a starting point, then the purpose of the opening chapter must be seen as introducing her. Verses 1-7 provide the necessary setting for her to enter the story, while vv. 8-18 begin to develop her character through three exchanges (vv. 8-10, 11-14, 15-18). Verses 1-7 introduce famine and death. Lack of food in Judah has forced an Israelite family to migrate to Moab. Once there the husband dies, the sons marry Moabite women, and then they also die. By v. 5 the story has been pared down to three widows, one of whom is a resident alien. This is not a promising situation for any of the women, but it is clearly a dead end for Naomi. The setting ends with a rumor of life in Judah because of the cessation of famine, and Naomi prepares to return. Verses 8-18 include three exchanges between Naomi and her two daughters-in-law, Orpah and Ruth. In the first two speeches Naomi is the principle speaker. First (vv. 8-10), she releases her daughters-in-law from any responsibility of returning to Judah with her by encouraging them to go home, to which they respond, No! Second (vv. 11-14), she underscores the absurdity of their response by emphasizing how there is no possible future for either of them if they accompany her back to Judah—if she got pregnant that very day, the two adult women could not marry the infants nor wait for them to grow up. The second argument gives rise to a split. Orpah leaves, but Ruth still remains. This separation is not a negative commentary on Orpah. Rather it underscores the nearly fanatical action of loyalty by Ruth. She is clinging on to nothing tangible. In this context she becomes the speaker of the third speech (vv. 15-18), where she claims undying loyalty to Naomi, her people, and her God; and then concludes the speech by swearing an oath in the name of her new God.

Two central points can be explored in preaching this text. Both have to do with the character of Ruth. The first is the power of Ruth's commitment to Naomi, even when there is nothing to gain, and everything to lose. When viewed in this way she certainly becomes an ideal of faith. By confessing that she would follow Naomi and her God at any cost Ruth turns what had only been a rumor of divine activity in vv. 6-7 into a reality. A second point builds off the use of the book of Ruth in Jewish worship. Here the Moabite background of Ruth stands out. In celebrating the Feast of Weeks and the giving of the law in Judaism, it is noteworthy that the non-Israelite Ruth is idealized. There is a profound insight here in Jewish-Christian relations that is worthy of reflection in preaching this text. Too often in Christian tradition Judaism is stereotyped as being exclusive in its focus over against Christianity, which is then viewed as being inclusive. The celebration of the Moabite Ruth in the Jewish equivalent of the Christian Pentecost certainly calls into question such prejudice, and the preaching of Ruth provides an excellent opportunity for the preacher to underscore this fact.

The Response: *Psalm 146*

A Hymn

Setting. Psalm 146 is part of a group of psalms including 146–150 that are characterized by the opening word, *hallelujah*. It is a hymn of praise, most likely of an individual.

Structure. The psalm is best separated into four parts. Verses 1-2 are an opening vow to praise God. What then follows is both negative (vv. 3-4) and positive (vv. 5-9) reflection on power. The hymn closes in v. 10 with an affirmation of God's rule in Zion.

Significance. The central two sections of the hymn provide the contrast that gives rise to praise of God. Trust in mortals can only lead to death. In contrast to this trust in humans, trust in God is secure, because the Creator is reliable. Once this security has been established in vv. 5-6, the remainder of this section describes the kind of power that emanates from God: justice for the oppressed, as well as care for strangers, widows, and orphans. These final images may be why this psalm of praise is associated with the opening chapter of Ruth. In any case the psalm is certainly meant to provide further commentary on Ruth's confession to Naomi that she would follow her and her God regardless of the circumstances.

New Testament Texts

The lessons deal with "the great sacrifice" and "the great commandment." Both passages are concise units. Hebrews presents a pointed argument about the superiority of the Christian covenant, while Mark recalls a telling conversation between Jesus and a scribe "not far from the kingdom of God." Remarkably, both lessons comment in different ways on the value of cultic offerings and sacrifices.

The Epistle: *Hebrews 9:11-14*

"How Much More . . . the Blood of Christ"

Setting. The third major section of Hebrews is 8:1–10:18. Here the author employs portions of Exodus 25–26 (a description of the Tabernacle), Psalm 40 (a promise to do God's will rather than merely offer formal sacrifices), and Jeremiah 31 (the well-known promise of a new covenant) to discuss the superiority of heavenly reality over its earthly copy. The theme of this part of the letter is the validity of the new covenant in Jesus Christ. A crucial ingredient in the argument is the contrast of the sacrifices of the old covenant with the sacrifice of Christ upon which the new covenant is founded.

Structure. In essence this passage is a declaration about the saving work of Jesus Christ. The author refers to Christ who "came as a high priest of the good things that have come" and explains that "through the eternal Spirit" Christ "offered himself without blemish to God."

Thus, as the foundation of the new covenant, Christ is both high priest and sacrifice. In our lesson the author develops this confessional position by constructing a series of explicit and implicit contrasts between the new and the old: (1) Christ passed through the greater and perfect tent—not made with hands, not of this creation; (2) Christ entered once for all into the Holy Place—not repeatedly as was necessary before; (3) Christ came to the Holy Place with his own blood—not that of goats and calves or that of goats and bulls and the ashes of a heifer; (4) Christ achieved eternal redemption—not necessarily repeated acts of atonement; (5) Christ purified the conscience of believers—not merely their flesh; and (6) Christ's purification produces the worship of the living God—not merely a series of dead works. At the heart of this argument is the issue of "blood."

Significance. A man with a pure book-knowledge of Judaism, an Old Testament book-knowledge at that, once visited a synagogue in Newport, Rhode Island. After looking around carefully, he found the rabbi and asked to see where the sacrifices were performed. In part, this incident illustrates how foreign a passage such as our lesson is to twentieth-century persons. We can easily grasp the basic point of the author's argument about the superiority of both Christ and the Christian covenant, but in fact we have no real-life experience in relation to which to interpret what the author says with his sacrificial metaphors. To make matters worse, the images from Judaism are pre-first century (notice the author refers to the tent, not to the Temple), and they represent a strong Hellenistic mixture of Judaism and Greek philosophy (notice the contrasts between the perfect heavenly realities and the imperfect earthly copies, a modified Platonic dualism).

The central image in this passage, "the blood of Christ," is especially difficult to comprehend. We understand the author's contentions that Christ is superior to the old high priests and that the redemption he achieves is superior to that brought through the practices of the old cult. But the key to his argument about superiority is "the blood of Christ." Readers are tempted to translate this phrase immediately as "Christ's death" or "Christ's self-sacrifice," and while both of these ideas are to be associated with "the blood of Christ," they do not provide adequate explication.

The author is working with a set of religious assumptions about

119

"clean and unclean." He takes the human dilemma, separation from God and the need of redemption, with utter seriousness, as would have other ancients. What has the power to purify humans from the defilement of sin? Only blood! Why? Because blood was regarded as the seat of the power of life itself by ancients. The author will write in 9:22-23:

> Indeed, under the law almost everything is purified with blood, and without the shedding of blood there is no forgiveness of sins. Thus it was necessary for the sketches of heavenly things to be purified with these rites, but the heavenly things themselves need better sacrifices than these.

The author contends that Christ, the Son of God, the one without sin, provided his own heavenly blood to establish the new, eternal redemption that purifies the very conscience of humanity for the service of the living God. The life of Christ held the needed power for the purification necessary to establish a new and lasting relationship between God and humankind. Christ brought the power of heavenly life not otherwise available and freely gave even himself to effect God's eternal redemption of humanity. If this strikes the modern mind as "far out," the author would respond that only something "not made with hands," something "not of this creation" can establish the eternal, perfect redemption that is the foundation of the new covenant.

The Gospel: *Mark 12:28-34*

No Commandment Greater Than These

Setting. In Mark's account, Jesus comes to Jerusalem prior to his Passion. Having arrived, he does and says a number of very striking things. This pre-Passion Jerusalem activity is recorded in 11:1–12:44. Here, Mark seems to have collected and arranged materials basically related to the Temple and to Jesus' dealings with the Temple authorities. In this cluster of stories, our lesson fits—but it also stands in contrast to the other incidents. This is the only story in the Gospel where a scribe takes a positive approach to Jesus and it produces a positive result. This moment is accentuated by occurring in a conspicuously hostile setting.

Structure. The scribe comes upon Jesus debating with the Temple authorities, and he makes opportunity for discussion himself. The story essentially reports a conversation: The scribe asks a question; Jesus replies; the scribe pronounces his opinion of Jesus' answer; and Jesus declares his verdict on the scribe. In the exchange, however, we find several striking elements. First, Jesus answers more than the scribe asked him. After replying to the scribe's question, Jesus gives more information that is not necessary in relation to the original question; and, then, Jesus makes a pronouncement over his own answers. Second, the scribe offers his assessment of Jesus' answer(s), and he unnecessarily repeats much of what Jesus said. Then, he makes a pronouncement that is unnecessary but quite telling. Third, Mark gives the reader insight into Jesus' own thinking about the statement of the scribe, and after Jesus makes his final pronouncement, we learn that no one dared to question Jesus further.

Thus, the story states and repeats the first and greatest (and the second!) commandment. At the same time, we are given an assessment of the value of "offerings and sacrifices." Throughout the whole story, Jesus acts with an awe-inspiring insight and authority. In reverse order these elements guide the following comments.

Significance. Jesus' answers to the interrogation of hostile questioners usually confounded them into silence and compounded their hostility. But, in this story, Jesus' very positive words about the scribe precede Mark's note that no one dared ask further questions. The insight Jesus shows into the commandments, into the scribe, and into the Kingdom are a bold demonstration of his authority. Who but God alone actually knows the location of the Kingdom and the proximity of any human to it? Jesus' knowledge goes beyond legalities and human nature to the real will of God, and his aplomb in pronouncing an assessment from the divine point-of-view should not be missed or underestimated. Mark's Gospel tells the reader that this Jesus is the Son of God, and as we encounter him in this story, his demeanor and his ability should reinforce Mark's identification of him.

The scribe is also a remarkable character. He seems to recognize in Jesus one who is worthy of conversation. The question he asks Jesus was one often put to prominent rabbis, to see how succinctly they could express the essence of the law. When this scribe recognizes the validity of Jesus' reply, he adds remarks about the relationship of the heart of the commandments and the cultic practices of religion that show he understands that true faithfulness to God's will is not captured or exhausted by mere religious ritual. God's will has to do with our relationships to God and to one another, and these relationships have everything to do with each other. There is no love of God that is reducible to practices unrelated to the dynamics of human existence. Right ritual can never take the place of real, loving relationships.

Not only does Jesus talk about loving God with heart, soul, mind, and strength and about loving our neighbors as ourselves, Jesus puts flesh on these commandments in the course of his own life. As we follow him through Mark's account, especially up to and through his Passion, we see what it means to love God and our neighbors with all that we are. In his words, Jesus offers us the central facts of true religion, and with his life he makes his teaching come true; thus, Jesus unifies knowledge and life-style, revealing what divine "facts and acts" look like in their right combination.

Proper 26: The Celebration

Today's Gospel lesson calls to mind the Summary of the Law, which used to follow the reading of the Decalogue at the beginning of many Reformed and Anglican liturgies. It might be employed today to set the tone for the service as part of the entrance rite. At the conclusion of the opening hymn, the minister faces the congregation and says:

THE CALL TO CONFESSION

Remember what our Lord Jesus Christ said: "You shall love the Lord your God with all your heart, and with all your soul, and with all your mind, and with all your strength," and, "You shall love your neighbor as yourself." Let us confess our sins against God and our neighbor. [silent recollection and confession]

PRAYER FOR FORGIVENESS

Lord Jesus,
you came to reconcile us to God and to one another.
Lord, have mercy. [sung or said]

Lord Jesus,
your blood heals the wounds of sin and division.
Christ, have mercy.

Lord Jesus,
you intercede for us with your Father.
Lord, have mercy.

DECLARATION OF PARDON OR WORDS OF ASSURANCE
PRAISE RESPONSE or PRAYER OF THE DAY

The Lord be with you.
And also with you.
Let us pray. O God, you have taught us to keep all your commandments
by loving you and our neighbor: Grant us the grace of your Holy Spirit,
that we may be devoted to you with our whole hearts, and united to one
another with pure affection; through Jesus Christ our Lord, who lives and
reigns with you and the Holy Spirit, one God, for ever and ever. **Amen.**

The service then continues with the first lesson. The Prayer for
Forgiveness is adapted from the Roman Catholic Sacramentary and
the collect is from the American Book of Common Prayer.

Today's psalm is available in a metrical paraphrase by Isaac Watts,
"I'll Praise My Maker While I've Breath" (*The Baptist Hymnal*, 1991,
no. 35; *The Mennonite Hymnal*, no. 25; *The Presbyterian Hymnal*, no.
253; *The United Methodist Hymnal*, no. 60). The emphasis in Hebrews
suggests William Cowper's "There Is a Fountain Filled with Blood."
Preaching on Hebrews can acquaint the congregation with the source of
the imagery of this hymn that is usually sung with much vigor and little
understanding. It can be found in most standard gospel hymnals and in
the following denominational books: *The Baptist Hymnal*, 1991, no.
142; *The Hymnbook* (Presbyterian), 1955, no. 276; *The United
Methodist Hymnal*, no. 622.

Today will frequently be observed by tradition in many churches as
Reformation Sunday, because it will be the Sunday closest to October
31. Preachers whose congregations observe this day may wish to ask
how the lessons can be used to address the issues of division and unity.
It is important for Protestants to be reminded that reformation is an
ongoing process, reformed and always reforming, and that this
reformation is one in which the entire Church participates. Liturgy and
sermon should rejoice in the ecumenical character of the day rather
than turning it into a sectarian festival of self-justification. In the
intercessions, local and regional leaders of denominations other than
one's own should be mentioned by name.

All Saints
November 1 or the
First Sunday in November

Old Testament Texts

Isaiah 25:6-9 describes a divine banquet on Mount Zion, and Psalm 24 is an entrance hymn.

The Lesson: *Isaiah 25:6-9*

A Banquet on Zion

Setting. Isaiah 25:6-9 is best characterized as being apocalyptic. A previsional understanding of apocalypticism is possible by contrasting this form of prophecy with classical prophecy in regards to both their theological outlooks and the distinct social milieu that have given rise to each.

A central feature of classical prophecy is a correspondence between the visions and words of the prophet and the present social system. This means that even though prophets were frequently critical of either the king or some other aspect of Israelite life, there was always an assumption that their message could prompt immediate change. Two insights concerning classical prophecy follow from this. The first is theological. Classical prophets understood God to be involved intimately both in the life of Israel and in the larger events of history. The second insight is sociological. The assumption of classical prophets that an oracle could instantly change behavior calls into question a common perception of prophets as being outsiders without real power in the ongoing social life of Israel. Classical prophets had real social power, and their criticism could change the policy of the king.

Apocalypticism is a complex development whose origin and influence in later Israelite religion are still under study, and the reader is encouraged to investigate the large body of literature on the topic. For our purposes apocalypticism will be characterized by contrasting it to the theology and sociology of classical prophecy. Theologically, apocalyptic literature does not share the confidence that God is involved in the day to day life of the people of God, and it does not assume that God is directing ongoing world events. We might say that apocalyptic literature is less optimistic about the degree to which God's salvation can be realized in the present time and about the purposefulness of history. This lack of optimism is usually reinforced by the social context of apocalyptic writers. Unlike classical prophets, these writers were usually in a position where they could not influence the social policy or the beliefs of the larger worshiping community. Apocalypticists, therefore, tended to be outsiders, yet they maintained the faith. In view of this the theological focus of apocalypticism tends to be on the distant future, where God is perceived as breaking into the present evil world, destroying it, and fashioning a new one, in which only the faithful would dwell. The imagery illustrates how apocalypticism is a disjunctive form of faith. It is disjunctive because belief in the salvation of God is maintained, even though all of life's experience states that such a faith could not possibly be true. With this as background it is easy to see how the resurrection of Jesus in the early church was formed in the larger context of apocalypticism. Our focus is on an earlier example of apocalyptic writing, Isaiah 25:6-9.

Structure. Isaiah 24–27 is often considered to be a self-contained unit with the book of Isaiah, because a great deal of the imagery within it turns to end-time visions of salvation. Isaiah 25:6-9 fits well into the context of Isaiah 24–27 because it provides an end-time vision of God hosting a banquet on Mount Zion. The text separates into at least two parts. Isaiah 25:6-8 describes the salvation that will take place on Mount Zion. This section has close links to Isaiah 24:21-23 where God's defeat of heavenly and earthly enemies is described, and where the reign of God on Mount Zion is specifically stated. The opening reference to "this mountain" in 25:6 links the two passages even more closely because it is meant to refer back to Mount Zion in 24:23. Isaiah 25:9 begins a new section that continues through v. 12. This section includes a song of thanksgiving in vv. 9-10a and a description of the destruction of the Moabites in vv. 10b-12. The extension of the song of thanksgiving through v. 10a provides a strong reason to expand the lectionary text to include at least the hymn in vv. 9-10a.

Significance. Apocalyptic literature is frequently characterized by an extensive use of mythology. The vision of salvation in apocalyptic literature is normally cosmic in scope (usually including a new creation), for which ancient Near Eastern mythology provided a vast reservoir of images. Three features of Isaiah 25:6-9 become clearer when they are viewed in the larger context of ancient Near Eastern mythology.

First, the setting of Mount Zion. Most gods live on mountains. Mount Olympus as the home of Zeus in Greek mythology comes to mind. In closer proximity to Israel, we could mention the Canaanite god Baal who lived on Mount Zaphon. The ancients believed that temples provided the channel where God was able to enter our world, and the imagery of elevation associated with mountains was meant to communicate this belief. The Lord is connected with a number of mountains in the Old Testament (Mount Sinai, Mount Moriah, Mount Horeb), but perhaps the most prominent mountain home for God is Mount Zion. Mount Zion has a specific geographical location in Jerusalem, where it referred to the Temple, but the symbol goes beyond reference to the Temple to envisage a whole new world in which God is present. An early example of the relationship between Temple and world occurs in Psalm 48:1 where the psalmist moves easily between specific geography and mythological or cosmological imagery in referring to Zion. Note how at one minute Zion is in "the city" where the Temple is located, and, then, how it is located in "the far north," which in Hebrew is the word *Zaphon*, Baal's mountain home. The reference to "the far north" goes beyond geography in order to envision a qualitatively different world, in which God is present. Vestiges of this kind of use of geography carry over in modern life in our reference to Santa Claus, who, we state confidently, also lives in the far north. If you have a small child who wants to get in the car and drive north to see Santa, then you know first hand, how reference to geography can become a symbol about a qualitatively different kind of world. This is also true of Zion. Although it described a specific mountain in Jerusalem, it also encompassed a vision of a new world order. We might summarize our discussion in the following way: mountains symbolize temples, because the latter were confessed to be the point where heaven and earth meet, with the result that God could be present with the worshiping community. Modern church steeples symbolize the same belief. The setting of the mountain is essential for interpreting Isaiah 25:6-9.

Second, the content of the vision. Two things happen in this vision: (1) God hosts a banquet on Mount Zion, and (2) God defeats death. Both of these events are firmly rooted in Canaanite mythology, where Baal hosts a banquet for the gods on his holy mountain, Zaphon, after he constructs his temple. In the larger structure of Canaanite mythology, Baal's banquet must be interpreted as his momentary defeat of death, or least chaos symbolized as the god Yamm. The writer of Isaiah 25:6-9 has taken over these images from Canaanite mythology to make a theological statement about the power of God to re-create and to save. If we take seriously the theological and social context of apocalyptic literature outlined above, then we must recognize that these powerful images of an end-time salvation are not an affirmation of experience, but a call to faith in spite of experience. This interpretation is supported by the song of thanksgiving in vv. 9-10a. This song is not an affirmation of the experience of the present worshiping community, but is placed in the future time ("It will be said on that day."). The language of the song indicates that the present worshiping community is best characterized as waiting for a salvation that is not yet realized. The result of this future orientation is that the images of salvation in vv. 6-8 provide both hope for tomorrow and a springboard for critically evaluating today.

This is the same text as Easter for this year. Having the similar texts underscores the close relation between Easter and the celebration of All Saints in the life of the Church, since the celebration of saints presupposes the power of God on Easter. Easter celebrates the events of being able to have a banquet on Mount Zion, while All Saints shifts the focus somewhat to celebrate all Christians, past and present, who are members at the feast.

The Response: *Psalm 24*

An Entrance Liturgy

Setting. Psalm 24 displays strong liturgical characteristics. The language of the psalm suggests a procession that leads into the Temple. This is particularly evident through the questions in vv. 3 and 8. The question in v. 3 concerns who may enter the sanctuary, while v. 8 raises questions concerning the nature of God.

Structure. The psalm clearly separates into three parts. Verses 1-2 are a hymnic section that celebrates the creative power of God and his ownership of all aspects of the world. Verses 3-6 have been characterized as a Torah liturgy, in which the character of worshipers is outlined in a question-and-answer format. Finally, vv. 7-10 are a gate liturgy. Once again the question-and-answer format provides the context for describing the character of the enthroned God.

Significance. Psalm 24 provides a fitting response to the apocalyptic imagery of Isaiah 25:6-9, for it takes the cosmic scope of the prophetic vision and pulls it into the worshiping community. The setting of worship is essential for celebrating something so mythic as the ongoing life of all Christian saints, past and present.

New Testament Texts

These lessons are about resurrection, the transforming power of God that brings new life, and the glory of God's future. Both texts are powerful declarations of good news. The verses from Revelation are fully concerned with the future, though as a message about the ultimate revelation and accomplishments of God's glory at the end they are certainly meant to inspire hope for life before the end. The lesson from John is part of the story of Jesus' raising of Lazarus. The message of these verses is also related to the future, but in the way Jesus speaks and works in this story we see plainly that the eternal life that we inherit through the Resurrection is already present in the lives of believers as God's saving and transforming power at work through Jesus Christ.

The Epistle: *Revelation 21:1-6a*

Seeing the End and Knowing What It Means

Setting. The book of Revelation is a remarkable early Christian writing. It forms a fitting final document for the New Testament (and the Bible), for it testifies to that which is anticipated in all that went before—namely, the ultimate triumph of God. The work comprises three literary types. Dominantly Revelation is a piece of apocalyptic literature, but worked into this kind of writing are epistles (chapters 2 and 3) and several prophetic-style declarations (part of our lesson!). Discerning the style in which a section is written assists greatly in interpreting the various part of the whole.

The general segment of the book from which our lesson comes is a great vision of the end that is recorded in 19:1–22:5. More specifically, our text is part of the vision of the new Jerusalem and the final word of God, 21:1-8. This is the final vision in a series of visions reported throughout the larger section.

Structure. These six verses are loaded! First, John of Patmos, the seer of Revelation, beholds the new heaven and the new earth. Second, he observes the descent of the new Jerusalem. Third, as John watches, a voice from the throne interprets the twin-vision by declaring the nature of the new relationship established between God and humans at the end. And, fourth, "the one who was seated on the throne" gives John a command to write, and then, (fifth?) that same figure (God) declares the completion of the divine work of redemption.

Significance. The vision is actually a double vision, telling of the same divine work in two ways (vv. 1-2). The voice explains the meaning of the events (vv. 3-4) and the truth of the vision and its explanation are confirmed by God himself (vv. 5-6*a*).

The reporting of a vision is typical of apocalyptic literature, though, as we see, a prophetic declaration is reported in the course of John's telling of the vision. Indeed, apocalyptic literature is kin to prophetic literature, but it seems to come from a situation of persecution and to be directed to people who are ostracized in order to offer them an encoded world of bold assurance. The visions reported prior to this one are primarily negative, but this final vision is purely positive.

God's triumph that is promised at the end is nothing other than the completion of God's work of redemption. Yet, we should be careful to notice that redemption is not a way forward into the past, as if by forging ahead God could or would take us back to the Garden of Eden. Redemption establishes something that goes beyond all that went before. Even in the Garden when God walked with humans, God's home was not with them. Thus, current creation theologies celebrate a goodness that Revelation judges to be inadequate. The end toward which God is moving is not a mere renewal of the present creation, rather God brings forth a new cosmological context in which a new city exists that is home to both God and humanity.

The images of the vision and the words from the throne seek to speak of that which is unspeakable. What God promises is far more than a qualitatively advanced existence similar to the lives we now live. In the new creation there is no chaos, death, or despair; but life with God means more than the elimination of these negative elements of our current lives. Yet, even through vision and divine declaration, John can only tell of the new promised home of God and humanity by pointing out what will not be there rather than by telling of what is there (other than God and humans). The glories of the promised triumph go beyond the words and images that we can comprehend. Yet, the truth of the promise is confirmed by the very word of God. The promise of God is that in the end God will make his home among humans and evil will be eliminated, but in our wildest dreams we cannot even imagine the positive dimensions of our new life with God. All the goodness our minds can conjure is finally not good enough to comprehend the glory of God's life among us. Unfortunately, to try to say more than this is to attempt to say more than Revelation is prepared to help us say. Fortunately, this is one matter in which God clearly has the final say.

The Gospel: *John 11:32-44*

Believing and Seeing the Glory of God

Setting. The first half of John is often called "The Book of Signs," because it recounts several acts of Jesus that are designated "signs"—that is, they point beyond the striking deeds to the true identity of Jesus. These stories are thought to have had a life prior to their incorporation into the current context of the Gospel, and they are often large and essential free-standing narratives. The lesson is part of a larger passage, 11:1-54.

Structure. The complete story in John 11 divides into seven scenes, several of which, for preaching, are capable of standing independently or being grouped. The seven scenes are (1) Jesus receives news of Lazarus' illness (vv. 1-5); (2) Jesus and his disciples (vv. 6-16); (3) Jesus and Martha (vv. 17-27); (4) Jesus and Mary (vv. 28-32); (5) Jesus at the tomb (vv. 33-41*a*); (6) Jesus raises Lazarus (vv. 41*b*-44); and (7) the council's thinking about Jesus (vv. 45-54). The lesson for All Saints takes one verse from scene four and all of scenes five and six.

Significance. John uses few words to tell of Jesus' meeting with Mary. In reading of this encounter in the context of the whole story we should be aware that this meeting is very different from Jesus' earlier encounter with Martha, despite the initial words of the statements by the sisters being the same ("Lord, if you had been here . . . "). When Jesus met Martha she declared her confidence in his ability to help. Yet the power which she perceived was merely his ability to intercede with God; it was not his person or an inherent capacity. Thus, there was a misunderstanding. Jesus said Lazarus would rise, and Martha thought of final resurrection. In turn, however, Jesus spoke overtly about himself and declared that a believer's confidence of salvation is not merely for the future, but for the here and now in relation to Jesus. And so, Jesus refers to himself as "the resurrection and the life." This is more than a pleonasm. Christian life begins now and continues despite death, because the Christian invests faith in Jesus himself. In contrast to this vital encounter between Martha and Jesus, Mary shows no overt confidence in Jesus' present power to help. Thus, Jesus observes her weeping and is deeply disturbed, but there is no dialogue about resurrection and life that points to Jesus as the source of eternal life.

When Jesus sees the mourners John tells us of his further distress and anger (vv. 33, 38). The atmosphere of grief and mourning are characteristic of a complete lack of faith. Notice, however, that Jesus himself was sorrowful. Yet, the Greek text contrasts the weeping of the crowd and the weeping of Jesus. The crowd "weeps and wails" (Greek, *klaiō*)—*a kind of formal funeral behavior; whereas Jesus "cries" (Greek, dakryō)*—a spontaneous bursting into tears! Jesus' tears are certainly for the suffering of Lazarus, but they are also for the human situation of darkness, which leads to such faithless behavior.

The crowd superficially recognizes Jesus' tears and reacts sympatheti-
cally, but with no understanding of who he is.

In the final segment of our lesson Jesus prays and gives an explicit
theological explanation for his activity. One striking feature of Jesus'
prayer is its opening; he says, "Father, I thank you for having heard
me." The words reveal that Jesus had already prayed about this
matter. Thus, we can understand that everything Jesus does and says
in this story (both his words and deeds strike the other characters in the
story as odd—see v. 37) is done out of Jesus' communion with God,
so that his activities reveal the will of God in operation. The
bystanders hear Jesus and are thereby exhorted to faith. Then, the
raising comes! The boldness of Jesus' voice and his command to the
crowd demonstrate his power and majesty. Overtly the dead Lazarus
is raised to life through the power of God working through Jesus.

The message at the heart of this story comes in Jesus' question in
v. 40, "Did I not tell you that if you believed, you would see the glory
of God?" The eyes of faith perceive the glorious, gracious, life-giving
work of God in actions that strike the eyes of the world as peculiar. For
persons of faith the power of eternal life that promises resurrection
operates already in our world and lives in the person of Jesus Christ
who embodies and reveals God's glory.

All Saints: The Celebration

All Saints Day is the Church's Memorial Day, a time to remember
those who have died in the faith of Christ. It is traditionally celebrated
on November 1, but may be observed on the first Sunday in November
instead. For Protestants, for whom the observance of saints' days may
be problematic to begin with, it is important to understand that in the
strict sense of the word this is a festival in honor of the grace of Christ.
In the classical tradition, the Christian calendar was divided into two
patterns, the dominical cycle and the sanctoral cycle. The dominical
cycle included all Sundays and other days of the year that celebrated
and recalled the major events in the life of our Lord (hence
"dominical"). The sanctoral cycle emerged as the Church sought to
remember the witness of particular saints, especially martyrs, on the
day of their death (their heavenly birthday). Gradually, however, the

popularity of saints days tended to crowd out the days of the dominical cycle as the number of saints to be remembered grew. By the time of the Reformation only the most important days in the dominical cycle were not displaced by one of the saints, and so the reaction was to get rid of saints days altogether. Four hundred years later there is a growing appreciation of the witness of the saints and the appropriateness of remembering them on certain days. Many denominational calendars have now restored saints to the list, including very recent ones such as Martin Luther King, Jr., Dietrich Bonhoeffer, and Florence Nightingale. All Saints Day, however, is not a part of the sanctoral cycle. It is part of the dominical cycle (hence it can be transferred to the following Lord's Day), because in the last analysis it is not a celebration of the saints per se, but rather of the victory of the grace of Christ in the saints. We are celebrating what Christ has done in and through the witness of the saints through the ages.

The color white is appropriate for today, as is the celebration of Holy Communion. This can also be an opportunity to explore in the sermon the meaning of the creedal term "the communion of saints" in relation to the words of the eucharistic preface, "with . . . all the company of heaven we praise your name." The names of those who have died since the previous All Saints service may be read and remembered as part of the service.

The administration of Holy Baptism is particularly appropriate for today, since in baptism we make new saints, in keeping with the New Testament's understanding of the word *saints*. As we remember those saints who have gone before, so we also rejoice in God's provision that the gospel will not be left without witness as others are added to the apostolic company.

See Hoyt Hickman, Don E. Saliers, Laurence Hull Stookey, and James F. White, *The New Handbook of the Christian Year* (Nashville: Abingdon Press, 1992), pp. 259-67 for expanded suggestions for a full service for this day.

Proper Twenty-seven
Sunday Between November
6 and 12 Inclusive

Old Testament Texts

The lesson from Ruth includes sections of the second half of the book. In the first text, Ruth claims the levirate right of redemption from Boaz (Ruth 3), and in the second, the genealogy of Ruth and Boaz is written to include King David. Psalm 127 is a wisdom poem about establishing a family.

The Lesson: *Ruth 3:1-5; 4:13-17*

Risking Redemption

Setting. The lessons for this Sunday presuppose a progression of events in the story of Ruth. Chapter 1 (the lesson for Proper Twenty-six) set the stage for introducing the Moabite, Ruth, by sketching, first, how there was famine in the land of Judah necessitating migration to the land of Moab by the family of Elimelech, and, second, how death claimed all the males, leaving Naomi and two daughters-in-law, Ruth and Orpah. The chapter ends with Ruth choosing to accompany Naomi to Judah. Chapter 2 introduces a new setting, harvest time in Judah, and a new character, Boaz, who has family ties with Naomi. Ruth remains the central character in this chapter. She suggests to Naomi that she should glean in the fields for grain (2:2), which she does, bringing her into contact with Boaz. The setting of chapter 2 is very public. The meeting of

Ruth and Boaz is in the context of other workers. Yet this chapter sets the stage for the more private meeting of Ruth and Boaz at midnight on the threshing floor in chapter 3.

Structure. As was noted in the commentary on Proper Twenty-six, the book of Ruth separates into four scenes by chapters. Thus the lectionary text frames the second half of the book of Ruth. Chapter 3:1-5 introduces the third scene in which Ruth meets Boaz at night, while the genealogy in chapter 4:13-17 closes the final scene by sketching out the results of the marriage of Boaz and Ruth. The problem of limiting the lectionary reading to the assigned verses is that the central role of Ruth is lost, since Naomi is really the central character in 3:1-5. The preacher may wish to expand the lectionary to include at least vv. 6-13 if not the entire chapter. If the entire chapter is read, note how it separates into three parts: vv. 1-5 and 16-18 focus on Naomi and Ruth, while vv. 6-15 describe Ruth and Boaz.

Significance. The background for chapters 3–4 concerns Israel's levirate laws. Deuteronomy 25:5-10 provides an example of one version of this law. It requires that a man marry the wife of his deceased brother for the purpose of having children in order to carry on the family name. In this version of the law the responsibility to redeem a family is limited to brothers. The law is functioning in a larger context in the book of Ruth to include extended family, so that Boaz comes under its jurisdiction. The levirate law provides the setting for a range of sexual metaphors throughout chapter 3.

Naomi begins the episode in 3:1-5 by setting in motion a midnight tryst between Ruth and Boaz for the purpose of gaining security for Ruth. Her instructions in vv. 3-4 do not make explicit reference to the levirate law, but they may in fact incorporate marriage imagery, especially with the commands to wash, to anoint and to put on fine clothes. Once Ruth is at the threshing floor, Noami instructs Ruth to locate Boaz lying down, to uncover his feet, and to lie down with him. Again the instructions imply sexual imagery in a number of ways without explicitly stating as much. The Hebrew verb "to lie down" (*yašab*) can mean to have sexual intercourse as it does in English; the instructions "to uncover the feet" of Boaz may mean legs or genitals (for the latter meaning see, e.g., Judges 3:24; I Samuel 24:3, Exodus 4:25), while the use of "to know" in the description of Boaz as a kinsman (v. 2, *modaytanu*) and in Naomi's instruction to Ruth (v. 4, *weyadat*—NRSV, "observe the place") can have both intellectual and sexual meaning. The sexual imagery picks up the larger theme about rumors of life in Judah that prompted Naomi's return from Moab in the first place. The harvest confirmed this rumor with regard to the previous famine in the land of Judah. The second half of the book establishes a much more private setting to explore this theme with regard to offspring. The closing advice of Naomi to Ruth is that after she created the situation on the threshing floor, that she be passive and await the advice of Boaz.

The point of the text that must be pursued in preaching is that Ruth does not follow the advice of Naomi. This point can only be illustrated by expanding the boundaries of the text to include the tryst between Ruth and Boaz in vv. 6-15. Ruth follows Naomi's instructions to the letter in vv. 6-7. Then at midnight Boaz awakens to find a woman lying at his uncovered feet, which prompts the obvious question, Who are you? (v. 8). At this point Ruth does not await instruction by Boaz as she was commanded, but instructs him, with technical language about Israelite levirate redemption: You are the one with the right to redeem (NRSV, "you are the next of kin"). The secrecy at night, the importance of not being seen, the need to leave before others awake all highlight the risk of Ruth's action. Her discourse to Boaz provides commentary on why she would risk such an action. He is the one who has the obligation to renew the life of her family. Her explicit citation of the levirate marriage law illustrates the degree to which Ruth has accepted Naomi's God and customs as she swore to do in chapter 1. Boaz recognizes both the faith in Ruth's actions and the risk that such action entails, and thus he pursues the levirate laws the following morning, bringing the story to conclusion.

The Response: *Psalm 127*

The Power of God in Human Affairs

Setting. Psalm 127 is best characterized as a wisdom poem. It may in fact consist of two separate proverbs, the first in vv. 1-2 about the dangers of building a house without God, and the second in vv. 3-5 about the blessing of progeny. The two somewhat different focuses of the proverbs have given rise to debate about the original unity of the psalm. If the building of a house in vv. 1-2 is interpreted as a family then the two parts of the psalm do appear to relate.

Structure. The first proverb consists of two sayings in v. 1 that emphasize the importance of divine activity in establishing a house. The sayings are parallel in structure, each beginning with the phrase, "unless the Lord," and ending with the conclusion, "vanity." Verse 2 picks up the motif of vanity to emphasize how work outside of God is anxious toil. The second proverb in vv. 3-5 praises progeny.

Significance. Psalm 127 provides at least two points of contact with the story of Ruth. The first is rooted in the second proverb, where progeny is praised. This proverb follows closely the praise that Naomi received in chapter 4:14 at the birth of Ruth and Naomi's son. In fact some scholars have linked Psalm 127 and Ruth together because of this connection. The second point of contact is more theological than literary. God is not an active participant in the book of Ruth. Clearly the story is about conversion and providence in the life of Naomi, Boaz, and especially Ruth, but God enters the story only through characters' speech, which is usually a wish or a confession. Psalm 127 provides a more direct theological commentary on the story of Ruth, especially through the first proverb, with its parallel sayings that unless one builds on God one builds in vain. The story of Ruth illustrates the positive side of these proverbs, by showing how the actions of someone who chooses to build on God do in fact lead to productive conclusions. This positive conclusion is true not only of Ruth, but also of Naomi and Boaz.

New Testament Texts

Both lessons are concerned with the work of Jesus Christ. Hebrews focuses on his superior sacrifice, which is the foundation of the new covenant of God with humanity. Mark recalls Jesus' teaching in the Temple area after Jesus established his lordly abilities in theological give-and-take.

The Epistle: *Hebrews 9:24-28*

The Better Sacrifice of Christ

Setting. Readers are asked to consult the discussion of the setting of the epistle lesson for Proper Twenty-six for a general overview of the location of this week's reading from Hebrews. Our lesson is part of a clear paragraph, 9:23-28. Verse 24 begins an explanatory sentence related to the statement in v. 23, so that for clarity one may choose to begin the reading one line earlier than the lectionary suggests.

Structure. Verse 23 makes the point that the new superior covenant of heavenly things—that is, the Christian covenant—requires better sacrifices than did the old covenant. The lines of our text explain the superiority of the one sacrifice, the sacrifice of Christ himself, which underwrites the new covenant. Verse 24 points to Christ's superior position as a mediator in relation to God. Verses 25-26 state four ways in which Christ's offering is superior to the old offerings, Christ "appeared" as high priest (1) once for all, (2) at the end of the age, (3) to remove sin, (4) by the sacrifice of himself. Then, vv. 27-28 extend the christological focus of this illustration of the superiority of the new covenant by speaking of Christ's forthcoming second appearance in an analogy to human death and subsequent judgment.

Significance. The author continues to teach his readers, clearly seeking to establish the thorough superiority of the new covenant of Christ over the first covenant. A crucial conviction of the author, which he assumes his readers share, is that the quality of a covenant is directly related to the quality of the sacrifices that establish the covenant. While today the topics of covenant and sacrifices are not among our normal range of thoughts, we can understand the logic of the author since we do understand maxims such as "a chain is no better than its weakest link" and "a vow is no better than the one who spoke it." The author assumes that "the end" and "the means to it" are vitally related.

In our lesson the author bases his claim of superiority on three items: the present position of Christ, the character of his saving work, and the work Christ will do in the future. The argument here takes on pronounced eschatological tones. Along a temporal line, Christ's past act of sacrificing himself to deal with sin gives him a present place in God's presence in our behalf that means he will appear a second time to save those who are eagerly waiting for him. The sacrificial work of Christ lays a claim on our lives, gives us a new freedom from sin, and imbues us with hope as we orient ourselves toward the promise of the future that has been brought into existence because of all that Christ has done and is doing. The reality of the past and the reality of the future are always being drawn forward and shaped anew by the reality of Christ's future.

This passage is remarkable, for it works almost completely at the level of faith. It is written by a person of faith to persons of faith for the purposes of solidifying their faith. If one were to respond, "I don't believe this," the author could only say, "Then you are left with the endless repetitions of the sacrificial cycles of the first covenant." It is by faith (a topic that will be treated prominently in Hebrews 11) that the author holds that the death of Christ has saving power. He views that death as the pouring out of divine life to remove sin (not merely to treat it temporarily), at the end of the age (not merely in the course of time), once for all (not merely one of many times). Indeed, it is by faith that the author understands that the death of Christ has to do with more than the past and the present, it means he will have power in the future to save those who devote themselves to him. These lines are a bold declaration of Christian conviction and a word of hope to those whose own confidence may be imperiled, and in proclamation one should move with these lines to pursue such ends.

The Gospel: *Mark 12:38-44*

Not This Way But That Way

Setting. Please consult the discussion of the setting of the Gospel lesson for Proper Twenty-six for an overview of the segment of Mark in which this lesson occurs. In the course of Jesus' activity in Jerusalem, recorded in 11:1–12:44, there is a deliberately assembled sequence of four interrogations: Pharisees question Jesus and he answers (12:13-17), Sadducees question Jesus and he answers (12:18-27), a scribe questions Jesus and he answers (12:28-34), and finally Jesus asks a question which no one answers (12:35-37). Thus, Jesus convincingly displays his superiority over his challengers. With his contenders silenced and with his enigmatic question still unanswered, the verses of our lesson show how Jesus continues to work in the Temple precinct teaching through a negative pronouncement and a positive picture lesson. These stories are the final installment in Mark's account of the public ministry of Jesus.

Structure. Two clear units compose our lesson, and while they could stand independently, they are set in tandem and together illustrate the positive and the negative sides of the same basic point. Verses 38-40 warn against public shows of piety that mask wretched self-serving practices, thus warning against incongruous living. Verses 41-44 illustrate a genuinely unified life of piety that means selfless generosity in gratitude to God. The contrast between the pompous scribes and the modest widow invite illustration of both ways not to live and the way to live as persons with religious sensibilities.

Significance. Jesus joins a long line of Israel's finest in denouncing the parading of piety. He singles out four activities that are particularly reprehensible. The desires to have the best seat in the synagogue and to acquire the place of honor at a banquet need little explanation. But the image of walking around in long robes may not be immediately intelligible. "Long robes" were specially designed garments meant to cover one completely as a sign of modesty during prayer and the performance of certain rituals. Yet, according to Jesus, some people found a way to make the most of modesty! Imagine a pastor walking around the local mall in a pulpit robe topped off with a stole or members of the choir keeping on their robes for Sunday lunch at the best restaurant in town. It strikes us as absurd. But what about wearing a four-inch wooden cross to work? Or what about religious bumper stickers on automobiles? Where do we draw the line? How? Why?

Jesus offers some help on this issue by coupling the wearing of long robes with "and to be greeted in the marketplace." In the ancient world superior persons received greetings from their inferiors, and they did not offer them until others recognized their superiority by speaking first. Jesus condemns dressing in religious garb with the motive of establishing one's superiority through the deliberate show of religion. Jesus is not telling us to hide our faith, rather he is warning us about manipulating religion to manipulate others.

Verse 40 drives this point home. The flamboyant parade of piety for the purpose of self-aggrandizement is shown to be nothing more than a mask for callous self-service. In this world we should be chary of pompous piety, for Jesus says people parading their devotion are likely out to take advantage of those who are vulnerable. With this point in mind it takes little time and effort to draw up a long, sad list of illustrations from our world of those who fit Jesus' description. Yet, notice that Jesus has already pronounced their fate, so that we are free from having to take on that job ourselves.

Jesus' next teaching is done through a picture lesson. The point of this story about the poor widow with her two copper coins is made plainly by Jesus in v. 44. Unfortunately it is more difficult to illustrate the total, selfless devotion of the widow than it is to illustrate the discrepancy between the posturing and practice of the scribes. In part the difficulty is the result of the genuine modesty of such devotion. But reflection should call to mind examples of the kind of generous devotion Jesus identified as real giving. Yet, beyond this level of illustration, we should not miss the critical juncture at which Mark locates this particular story. The account of the widow who "put in everything she had, all she had to live on" immediately precedes the final dramatic episode of Mark's story of Jesus. In his Passion Jesus "put in everything," not only "all [he] had to live on," but even his very life.

The poor woman models for us the Christian pattern of stewardship of possessions. She shows us the manner in which we are to regard our belongings in relation to God. To be a Christian is to wear the name of Christ. If that name is a valid identification, our lives will testify, even at the level of material things, to the lordship of the one whose name is now ours. Like Jesus Christ, this woman was free in relation to God—free from fear in the face of this world's realities, and free for unbridled generosity in response to the goodness of God.

Proper 27: The Celebration

As we near the end of the Christian year the lessons begin to turn our thoughts to eschatological matters, to the end of time. Next week's Gospel reading will take us to the beginning of Jesus' apocalyptic discourse in Mark 13 where we began reading twelve months ago on the First Sunday of Advent. Today the epistle lesson contains the only explicit reference in the New Testament to a "Second Coming." Preachers who feel drawn to that text need to examine it very closely and separate clearly what the passage says from what they have been taught about a second coming. Notice immediately that the term *second coming* is not used. Jesus is spoken of as coming a second time (meaning, yet another time?) which is quite a different thing. We should admit up front that the author of Hebrews was an early Christian who lived with the expectation of an imminent parousia, but there is no evidence to suggest a belief in any kind of a real absence in which the presence of Christ is actually divorced from the Church on earth. The larger New Testament witness is that one may abandon belief in an imminent return without abandoning belief in both the abiding presence of Christ where two or three are gathered in his name and the promise that Christ will be there at the end of the age. A change in dating no way undermines the significance of the work of Christ as Hebrews presents it.

The commentary on the Gospel lesson makes clear that there is more to do with the story of the widow's mite than use it for Stewardship Sunday (which this day may be in many denominational program calendars). The issue is one of life-style and of self-oblation. The following hymn by Joachim Lange, translated by John Wesley, comments at a deeper level on the two pericopes that compose today's lesson. It may be sung to St. Catherine or Melita.

> O God, what offering shall I give
> to thee, the Lord of earth and skies?
> My spirit, soul, and flesh receive,
> a holy, living sacrifice:
> small as it is, 'tis all my store;
> more shouldst thou have, if I had more.
>
> Now, O my God, thou hast my soul,
> no longer mine, but thine I am;
> guard thou thine own, possess it whole,
> cheer it with hope, with love inflame;
> thou hast my spirit, there display
> thy glory to the perfect day.
>
> Thou hast my flesh, thy hallowed shrine,
> devoted solely to thy will;
> here let thy light for ever shine,
> this house still let thy presence fill;

O source of life, live, dwell, and move
in me, till all my life be love!

Send down thy likeness from above,
and let this my adorning be;
clothe me with wisdom, patience, love,
with lowliness and purity,
than gold and pearls more previous far,
and brighter than the morning star.

Lord, arm me with thy Spirit's might,
since I am called by thy great name;
in thee let all my thoughts unite,
of all my works be thou the aim:
thy love attend me all my days,
and my sole business be thy praise.

Even on Stewardship Sunday, the last line makes clear what the "bottom line" of the stewardship report should be.

Proper Twenty-eight Sunday Between November 13 and 19 Inclusive

Old Testament Texts

The two texts encompass the birth story of Samuel from two different perspectives. The lesson describes the circumstances leading up to the birth of Samuel in which barrenness is central. Here birth is viewed from the point of view of petition. The response, on the other hand, is praise by Hannah at the birth of Samuel.

The Lesson: *I Samuel 1:4-20*

Petition

Setting. Barrenness is a common motif in biblical tradition. It is frequently a problem for the matriarchs throughout Genesis. Sarah is barren, as is Rebekah and Rachel. Furthermore, barrenness is often placed in a larger context of rivalry either between two wives or between a concubine and a wife; in either case the barren woman is the favored one of the husband. Examples include Sarah and Hagar as well as Rachel and Leah. The birth story of Samuel fits this pattern in both parts. Hannah is barren as compared to Peninnah, who has many children, and Hannah is the favored wife of Elkanah. On a literary level the repetition of this motif tends to signal a significant birth. Thus, at the outset we expect the barren Hannah to become pregnant and to give birth to a significant character. On a theological level the motif of barrenness brings to mind God's promise of progeny to

Abraham in Genesis 12. This is certainly true of the repetition of the motif in Genesis. The repetition of so many details of this motif in the birth story of Samuel at the very least suggests that the authors of I Samuel may be inviting the reader to interpret Samuel's birth in the larger context of the ancestors in Genesis, and, more particularly, as a continuation of the divine promise to Abraham in Genesis 12.

Structure. First Samuel includes two yearly cycles of sacrifice at the Shiloh cult. It begins with Elkanah going up to Shiloh for sacrifice in one year (v. 3) and the chapter concludes with a repetition of this action the following year (vv. 21-28, or for Hannah sometime later, after Samuel was weaned). This repetition is important for it brings to light another repetition in structure that will aid our interpretation. Two times Hannah is presented as praying at the Shiloh cult. The Old Testament lesson in vv. 4-20 contains her first prayer in the initial year, which is a vow in v. 11. The psalm response of 2:1-10 is really the content of her prayer the second time she entered the Shiloh cult. The two Old Testament texts for this Sunday follow a progress in Hannah's prayers from petition to praise, from vowing to the fulfillment of a vow. The entire cycle, taken as a whole, provides a framework for preaching.

First Samuel 1:4-20 centers on petition and vow. The text separates into four parts. Verses 4-8 underscore the rivalry between Hannah and Peninnah; vv. 9-11 are Hannah's petition and vow to God at the Shiloh cult; vv. 12-18 include an exchange between Eli and Hannah; and vv. 19-20 narrate the birth of Samuel.

Significance. The rivalry between Hannah and Peninnah introduces a conflict that will become a structuring device in I and II Samuel. A series of characters will be pitted against each other (e.g., Samuel–House of Eli, Saul–David), with the seemingly weaker character emerging victorious over the more powerful. Although this is important background for interpreting the whole book of I Samuel, it is probably best not to emphasize this motif for preaching the opening chapter of Samuel. A better point of focus is the barrenness of Hannah. With this as a focus, the rivalry can be used to accentuate the degree to which barrenness is a problem for Hannah, which comes to expression in her prayer in vv. 9-11. The content of Hannah's prayer is a vow that if God would give her a child, she would give the child back to God as a Nazirite. There is irony when Eli enters the scene in vv. 12-18, because, while Hannah is committing a future son to the Nazirite vow, which included the abstinence from alcohol, Eli thinks that she is drunk. This lack of insight by Eli is probably meant to illustrate a character flaw, which is also carried over into his perception of his sons. This commentary on Eli is secondary to the text, however. What is important is that he functions in his role as priest by communicating an oracle of salvation: "Go in peace; the God of Israel grant the petition you have made to him." The concluding response of Hannah, that she rejoined her husband and was no longer sad, indicates her acceptance and confidence in the oracle of salvation in spite of her barrenness. The oracle of salvation, along with Hannah's act of faith lead to the birth of a son in vv. 19-20. The naming of the son as Samuel ("I have asked him of the Lord") underscores Hannah's perception of this birth as a divine response to her prayer.

The Response: *I Samuel 2:1-10*

Praise

Setting. Even though the Song of Hannah appears to have functioned at an earlier time independently of its present context (note, e.g., the reference to seven children in 2:5), nevertheless, it is now intimately interwoven into its present context—so much so, in fact, that the Song of Hannah must be read in the larger context of I Samuel 1 (note how I Samuel 1:21-28 is providing the context for Hannah's second prayer in 2:1-10). The unified context of I Samuel 1:1–2:10 underscores how Hannah is providing her own response to the Old Testament lesson (1:4-20), from the perspective of having experienced the fulfillment of her petition. The occasion for the song of praise is not when God answers Hannah's petition, but when Hannah fulfills her vow to give the son back to God.

Structure. First Samuel 2:1-10 can be categorized as a personal psalm of thanksgiving. Such psalms separate into four parts: an introduction of praise (vv. 1-2), a recounting of personal experience (vv. 3-5), which evolves into confession (vv. 6-7), and concludes with thanksgiving rooted in confidence.

Significance. The second prayer of Hannah must be interpreted in two ways: from the point of view of the content of the song and its context in the larger story. First, the content of the song. A personal psalm of thanksgiving has two functions, to praise God and to teach fellow worshipers about God in light of the personal experience of the singer or psalmist. The introduction (vv. 1-2) fulfills the first goal through a variety of motifs of thanksgiving. The second section of the psalm (vv. 3-5) provides the reason for praise by recounting personal experience in which the reference to child birth is now meant to be Hannah's experience. The third section (vv. 6-7) shifts from praise to teaching when a series of reversals are catalogued through antithetical parallelism (the Lord kills and gives life, brings low and raises up, makes poor and rich). These confessional conclusions arise out of the experience of the psalmist. The psalm ends (vv. 9-10) with praise rooted in confidence about God's ability to care for the people of God. In summary, the experience of Hannah is one of reversal in fortune, which provides insight into God and God's salvation.

Second the context of the song. When interpreting the psalm in its context note that Hannah's praise does not follow the birth of Samuel in I Samuel 1:19-20. Rather it takes place at a later time, when Hannah is actually giving up the child in order to fulfill her vow. Petition and vow must be held together in preaching this text. The problem of barrenness and the association of this motif to Genesis suggests that Hannah's petition for a child is rooted in a divine promise of progeny, which, if granted, will elicit a promise from her that the child will be given back to God. The interrelationship of petition and vow means that the story cannot end after the birth of Samuel. Rather, praise and thanksgiving is in the act of fulfilling the vow. There is a reversal here in the actions of Hannah that corresponds to the content of the hymn, since she is thanking God for the gift of a child by giving Samuel back to God. One point of the birth of Samuel when it is read from the perspective of Hannah is that salvation is an unexpected reversal, which when experienced and recognized, can prompt the same kind of reversal in ourselves. Such action is the content of praise to God.

New Testament Texts

The readings continue to move through Hebrews and Mark, but as we draw to the end of Year B the selections from Mark take a deliberate path into eschatological materials. Hebrews continues to meditate on the meaning of the great sacrifice of Christ, pondering the meaning of his death, resurrection, and exaltation as the basis of the new sin-free life of Christians.

The Epistle: *Hebrews 10:11-14 (15-18), 19-25*

Living Up to What God Has Done for Us in Jesus Christ

Setting. We encountered Hebrews 10 as the epistle lesson for Good Friday of Year B. The following discussion repeats parts of that earlier treatment.

Many commentators contend that the verses of our lesson are from both the ending of the third major section of Hebrews, which focuses on Christ's death (8:1–10:18), and the beginning of the fourth major section of the epistle which deals with the new and living way of faith for believers (10:19–12:29). Other interpreters regard the verses of this lesson as the closing segment of a larger section treating the meaning of Christ's great sacrifice and its application to Christian life (8:1–10:25). Whichever understanding one holds, it is the case that the text is located at or near a pivot in the epistle. Thus, the verses of the lesson present reflection upon both Christ's death and the meaning of that death as the basis of the new life of Christians.

Structure. We shall treat the full complement of the verses for this reading, for there are two general movements in the lesson. First, vv. 11-18 contrast the conduct of "every priest" at the inferior daily sacrifices with the conduct of Christ after the single superior sacrifice. The author moves through this christological metaphor to speak of the new covenant that is the fulfillment of God's promises. This covenant is presented as a divinely accomplished reality, and it is interpreted to mean that the old sacrificial system has been superseded and is, therefore, irrelevant. Second, vv. 19-25 seek to apply the teaching about the new covenant to the lives of the believers, saying that through the sacrifice of Jesus believers have access to holy space wherein their lives are purified and their relationships are redefined. Covenant freedom, Christ's sacrifice, and a new context and way of life are the themes of this lesson.

Significance. The two parts of the lesson correlate the accomplishments of God through Jesus Christ with the new manner of living of believers, basing the latter on the former and urging persons of faith to live up to what God has done for them. God is the covenant maker according to our lesson. Covenant is a pact, a compact, a mutually restricting and mutually beneficial agreement that forms the basis of a relationship between two parties. Remarkably, however, in relation to the new covenant of which our lesson speaks, God promised this covenant, God acted to effect this covenant, and humans basically derive benefits from what God has done, doing little-to-nothing themselves to establish this covenant! Pretty good news!

The opening verses of this lesson (vv. 11-15) reflect on Christ's sacrifice (death) and his preeminent priesthood, which is seen in his being seated in triumph after that sacrifice (resurrection-exaltation). Then, Hebrews uses the quotation from Jeremiah in vv. 16-17 to interpret the work of God in Christ to God's establishment of a new covenant. As the old covenant had sacrifices and priests, the new covenant has one sacrifice and one priest, the same Jesus Christ. Hebrews declares that the old covenant functioned externally in relation to its participants, but now we learn that one of the blessings of the new covenant is that God has worked through Jesus Christ to make the new covenant an internal affair, written on human hearts and, thus, transforming human lives. We do not merely live up to the conditions of the covenant of Christ, rather, because of its radical internal character, we live out of its powerful standards. All this means a newly given freedom for us as participants in the new covenant. Through Christ, God has established a new basis of relating to humans that frees us through absolute forgiveness. God's action in Christ frees us from the past to live into the freedom of God's previously promised and now fulfilled present and future.

Verses 19-25 issue a call to commitment by extending the metaphor of priestly sacrifice from the prior section(s). Now Hebrews expounds the meaning of Christian life through a since-this-then-that argument. To paraphrase, "Since because of the work of Christ we have a new relationship to God, then let us live in faith, let us live in hope, and let us live in a new relationship with one another." Christian freedom means a new life of confidence in God, a new life of expectation that

God will continue in an even greater way the work already begun, and a new selfless pattern of community life where we worship together and give mutual support to one another for the edification of the community of faith. With faith and hope in God, yielding a life of confidence and expectation, we are called together into a corporate life of celebration and realization of God's purposes.

The Gospel: Mark 13:1-8

Signs of the Times

Setting. Through the first twelve chapters of Mark's account we have followed Jesus' ministry from its origins in Galilee into Judea and, eventually, to Jerusalem. All along the way Jesus spoke and acted in an authoritative fashion, and he steadily debated with recognized religious authorities concerning the law and God's will. In Jerusalem the debates intensified (as we saw in the past few weeks' lessons) and Jesus' activities became more controversial. We find that his teaching becomes mysterious and startling. Now, Mark 13 forms a final section of teaching offered privately to the disciples. Jesus is particularly concerned with the future, and his remarks immediately precede the large complex of thoroughly integrated stories forming the Passion narrative (Mark 14 and 15 [and 16?]).

Structure. Chapter 13 is a cluster of teachings about the future. Scholars contend this material was not delivered as a single continuous lesson; rather the materials in this chapter seem to come from different times and settings. But the common concern of these teachings with the future led to their collection on the principle that "like attracts like." Mark offers the section as a grand final pronouncement before the great climax of the Passion; yet, there are distinguishable units of material in the whole.

At a glance—as suggested by the paragraphing of the NRSV—this week's lesson appears to fall into two clear-cut scenes, vv. 1-2 and vv. 3-11, which are logically sequential. But examination of the verses and reflection on the material suggests that there are three distinguishable parts to the lesson and that their relationship is peculiar. First, vv. 1-2 are set in the Temple precinct. The disciples remark on the stones of the buildings, and Jesus replies with a forecast of the Temple's destruction. Second, in vv. 3-4 the scene shifts to the Mount of Olives where four disciples query Jesus about the time and the signs of the temple's devastation. Third, Jesus speaks, but he does not so much comment on the fate of the Temple as he does on the trauma leading to "the end."

Significance. Part of the difficulty in interpreting Mark 13 is that the sections of this chapter deal with two distinct times of distress: the trauma of the destruction of Jerusalem and the crisis of final judgment at the end of time. Distinguishing these times from each other is a key to comprehending the message(s) in this lesson.

The strange but striking coupling of references to the Temple's destruction with statements about the trauma leading up to the end is Mark's way of saying that the dramatic end of time as a day of final divine judgment is as certain as the fate of the Temple in Jerusalem. The disciples in this account are riveted by Jesus' statements about the Temple, but when Jesus speaks he takes the conversation to a higher plane, looking through time toward the end which gives everything in time a relative value. International conflicts and natural catastrophes are distressingly real, but they come in the course of time and in comparison with the end—that is, in comparison with God's judgment of the cosmos—they are but the beginning of birthpangs.

Birthpangs intensify as labor proceeds. But Jesus says that compared to the trauma of the delivery of divine judgment at the end, the worst forms of human and natural disaster are like the initial unsettling twinges of light labor. Jesus understands that temporal crises are real, but he insists that they are not worthy of our ultimate concern. Rather than worry about the timing of future historical catastrophes, believers are to concern themselves with God's future.

Yet, even in calling for concern with God's end rather than human and natural time, Jesus insists that believers are not to be merely concerned with timing. It actually matters very little when the end will arrive. Instead of becoming preoccupied with the moment of the end, believers are to be aware of the danger of being led astray in the time prior to the end. The other portions of this eschatological discourse from Jesus make clear that believers are to be steadily ready for God's judgment, precisely because the time of the end is unknown. When people claim to know the time, they are not to be heeded; for to waste time in end-time speculations is to go astray from the essential life of faith to which Christ has called disciples.

Proper 28: The Celebration

The Old Testament commentary for Proper Twenty-six told us that in the Hebrew scriptures I Samuel immediately follows the book of Judges without the interposition of Ruth. The preacher may find it helpful then to introduce the reading from the beginning of I Samuel in light of the last verse in Judges: "In those days there was no king in Israel; all the people did what was right in their own eyes" (21:25). This sets the stage for the ministry of Samuel who anoints the first two kings of Israel. The ministry of Samuel is responsible for the transition from inter-tribal conflict and turmoil to the stability and peace that David finally brings. A parallel may be drawn between the conditions described in Israel at the end of the age of the judges and the conditions described by Jesus in the Gospel lesson concerning the end of the age. In each case God acts to inaugurate a new age, first under the kingship of David and now under the rule of "great David's greater Son." Hannah's song is a prefiguring of the Magnificat, which extols the radical character of God's rule and which we will be singing five weeks from today (see the entry for the Fourth Sunday of Advent, Year C).

The last section of the lesson from Hebrews may be used as a means of introducing various elements of the service. The entrance rite could include sprinkling water toward the congregation as a sign of forgiveness after the prayer of confession. The minister would then say to the people:

> Since we have confidence to enter the sanctuary
> by the blood of Jesus,
> by the new and living way that he opened for us,
> and since we have a great high priest over the house of God,
> let us approach with a true heart
> in full assurance of faith,
> with our hearts sprinkled clean from an evil conscience
> and our bodies washed with pure water.

The opening hymn of praise would then be sung.

The Creed or affirmation of faith may be introduced with these words:

Let us hold fast to the confession of our hope without wavering, for God who has promised is faithful.
Or it may be said by the minister after the Creed, and the people would respond, "Amen."

The following can serve as the dismissal accompanying the blessing at the end of the service:

Consider how to provoke one another to love and good deeds, continue to meet together, and encourage one another, as we await the approaching Day of the Lord.

Appropriate hymns for the day include "O Day of God, Draw Nigh" (*The Baptist Hymnal,* 1991, no. 623; Episcopal, *The Hymnal 1982,* no. 600-601; *The Presbyterian Hymnal,* no. 452; *The United Methodist Hymnal,* no. 730) and "O God of Earth and Altar" (*Baptist and Disciple Hymnbook for Christian Worship,* no. 373; Episcopal, *The Hymnal 1982,* no. 591; *Lutheran Book of Worship,* no. 428; *The Mennonite Hymnal,* no. 457; *The Presbyterian Hymnal,* no. 291; United Methodist, *Book of Hymns,* 1964, no. 484; *UCC Hymnal,* no. 187).

Proper Twenty-nine (Christ the King) Sunday Between November 20 and 26 Inclusive

Old Testament Texts

Second Samuel 23:1-7 is part of the last words of David that provide a closing to I and II Samuel. Psalm 131:1-12 (13-18) is a festival hymn that includes both dedication and prophetic admonition.

The Lesson: *II Samuel 23:1-7*

A Closing Divine Oracle

Setting. First and Second Samuel is framed by poetry. The Song of Hannah in I Samuel 2:1-10 introduces the book, while the Song of David in II Samuel 22:2–23:7 closes it. The Song of Hannah has two functions. It provides commentary on the experience of Hannah (vv. 3-8, the Lord is a God who brings about unexpected reversals in life), and it provides a prophetic statement about the future reliability of God, especially with regard to the king (vv. 9-11). The Song of David performs similar functions. The early poetry (II Samuel 22) is David's song of praise that arises from his experience of salvation, while II Samuel 23:1-7 moves into a more prophetic perspective like the conclusion of Hannah's song in I Samuel 2:9-11. But there is a change between the two songs at this point. The Song of Hannah presented a series of strong statements about God's protection of a future king. Second Samuel 23:1-7 is more ambiguous for a number of reasons. Although v. 5 clearly states the future reliability of God in supporting the king much like the conclusion to the Song of Hannah, it is difficult to determine how this reliability should be interpreted with regard to David. The problem is that although David is the speaker in II Samuel 23:1-7, he is actually conveying a divine oracle directed to him. In other words, he is both the speaker and the object of the speech. The question that this raises is whether the promise of v. 5 actually applies to David or is he being judged by it? The ambiguity of this closing hymn is an important factor for preaching this text.

Structure. The ambiguity noted above will become clearer through a study of the structure of II Samuel 23:1-7. Verse 1a encourages the reader to interpret vv. 1b-7 as David's last words. Yet within this unit vv. 1b-3a are not David's reminiscence. Instead these verses must be interpreted as divine speech in the genre of prophetic discourse. David's last words, therefore, are a soliloquy that contain a mixture of divine speech in vv. 1b-3a and his own words in vv. 3b-7, since David is clearly the speaker in v. 5 (note the first-person references—such as, "my house"—and the third-person references to God—such as, "he has made with me," or "will he not cause to prosper all my help"). Verses 3b-4 and 6-7 are less clear as to who the speaker is because they are wisdom sayings. Consequently they can be read in two ways. As conclusions by David about the nature of kingship at the close of his reign, or as prophetic divine speech directed to David, in which case the wisdom sayings provide a standard by which David must be judged.

Significance. Two problems of interpretation arise in II Samuel 23:1-7 that are important for preaching this text. The first is why wisdom sayings are offered as the content of prophecy at the close of David's life. The second problem concerns the translation of v. 5. We will begin with the second problem.

Verse 5 separates into three parts: an opening question or affirmation introduced by the Hebrew phrase *ki lo'* (NRSV, "Is not my house like this with God?"), the recounting of the everlasting covenant with David (NRSV, "For he has made with me an everlasting covenant, ordered in all things and secure."), and a closing question or affirmation introduced by the phrase *ki lo'* (NRSV,

"Will he not cause to prosper all my help and my desire?''). The problem of interpretation of this verse can be stated as follows. Is v. 5 an affirmation by David that he has indeed fulfilled the proverb in vv. 3b-4 about a just ruler? Or is v. 5 a question of doubt by David that he has fallen short of the standard of the proverb? The ambiguity arises from the Hebrew construction *ki lo'* (literally translated, because/for not). Some translators interpret this construction as indicating emphasis (thus having an asseverative function like "certainly not") in which case the opening line of v. 5 would be translated, "Yes, my House stands firm with God" (as in The Jerusalem Bible). Other translators interpret the construction as an expression of doubt or at the very least as a negative rhetorical question, "Is not my house like this with God?" (NRSV). The problem of how to translate the opening line returns at the close of the verse where a second question is introduced with *ki lo'*. What is at stake in the debate is the role of David in the context of the divine oracle. Is he being affirmed by it or judged by? The ambiguity in the very syntax of the verse suggests both.

The use of the wisdom sayings as the content of prophecy further encourages the ambiguity of David's last words. The elaborate prophetic introduction prepares us for a more explicit prophetic speech, such as , "Thus says the Lord to David. You have ruled the people justly. . . . " But we don't get such direct speech. Instead we get a more detached statement about what a just king ought to be like, without the specific name David being attached to the saying. It is the detachment of the wisdom saying, which forces David to apply it to himself in v. 5. Yet when we get to this crucial verse, we don't get a clear answer. What in fact does he say? And this ambiguity leads to a larger problem. How do we preach texts which seem to lead us into such conundrums? A good rule of thumb for interpretation is that such ambiguity is not an accident, but the point of the text. If we follow this rule, then the central question for interpretation must be: What is the message in having David's last words yield two meanings—doubt and confidence?

At the very least, biblical writers are saying that the story of David is a story of divine promise working itself out in human affairs. This is made clear in the recitation of the unconditional covenant in v. 5. (The setting of a prophetic oracle reminds us of the introduction of this promise in II Samuel 7, which also occurred by means of a prophetic oracle by Nathan.) Unconditional divine covenants, however, are very dangerous things in the hands of humans, since such confessions often encourage us to equate the events of our lives too easily with divine destiny. The ambiguity of David's last words addresses this danger, for it leaves unresolved whether God's unconditional covenant with David is a source of judgment or assurance for him at the end of his life. Are his last words an expression of doubt or confidence? The reason for this final uncertainty is that the wisdom saying (which in this context is God's final revelation to David) actually stands over against the person, providing a clear standard by which David can answer the question.

By structuring David's final words in such a way (the character who is most closely associated with divine destiny in the Old Testament), the writers of II Samuel 23:1-7 seem to be suggesting that we evaluate divine destiny in our lives and larger society by objective standards of divine wisdom rather than on the basis of our own life experience or certain heroic individuals around us, since all humans in the end are judged by the same divine standards. The point of the text is that divine destiny is more the working out of certain standards in this world to which God is unconditionally committed and that the degree to which humans participate in these standards (even David) is the measure by which we will be evaluated.

The Response: *Psalm 132:1-12 (13-18)*

Divine Promise to the King

Setting. Psalm 132 recounts some form of a ritual in Israel's pre-exilic period. The ritual probably included a procession with the Ark. Note how the Ark is referred to in v. 8: "Rise up, O LORD, and go to your resting place, you and the ark of your might." The ritual procession of the Ark, however, certainly goes back to v. 6, where the hymn is interrupted by a chorus (note the first person plural *we*) who describes finding the Ark in the field of Jaar, before bringing it to the Temple for worship in v. 7. The content of the psalm would suggest that the ritual is a celebration of the Lord's election of both the king and the Temple in Jerusalem.

Structure. The structure of Psalm 132 is difficult to determine and the reader is encouraged to consult other commentaries for a variety of possibilities. One of the simpler structures that has been proposed is that the psalm divides between vv. 1-10 and 11-18, in which case the first part of the psalm is an appeal to the Lord to remember past promises to David and Zion, and the latter part consists of the divine answer. If this structure is followed, then the lectionary text must be adjusted to include only vv. 1-10 or the entire psalm.

Significance. Psalm 132 explores how the divine promises of election can be appropriated in worship. The first part of the psalm uses the tradition of David's election as a basis for language of petition. Verses 1-10 begin with a call for God to remember past promises as well as the faithfulness of David and this unit ends with a request that God not turn away from the petitioner precisely because of these past promises. The second part of the psalm both recounts God's past promises to dwell in Jerusalem and reaffirms the power of these promises in the present worshiping community.

New Testament Texts

These lessons are remarkably different from each other, but careful reading will show that both deal with the theme of the heavenly character of the ultimate goal of Christian belief and practice. Moreover, while Revelation and John present Jesus Christ from their own points of view—Revelation as "the faithful witness, the firstborn of the dead, and the ruler of the kings on earth" and John as "the King of the Jews" whose "kingdom is not from the world" and who "came into the world to testify to the truth"—both lessons have a crucial christological focus.

The Epistle: *Revelation 1:4b-8*

God's Grace and Peace Through Jesus Christ

Setting. The book of Revelation is a remarkable early Christian writing. It is a fitting final document for the New Testament (and the Bible), for it testifies to that which is anticipated in all that went before—namely, the ultimate triumph of God. The work comprises three literary types. Dominantly Revelation is a piece of apocalyptic literature, but worked into this kind of writing are epistles (chapters 2 and 3) and several prophetic-style declarations (part of our lesson!). Discerning the style in which a section is written assists greatly in interpreting the various part of the whole.

The verses of our lesson come after the title and introductory statement at the outset of Revelation (vv. 1-3). Remarkably, our lesson casts the beginning of Revelation in the form of the opening of a typical Hellenistic letter, a style well-known from the epistles of the New Testament.

Structure. The standard beginning of a Hellenistic letter had three parts: (1) Salutation—"Sender" to "Recipient"; (2) Greeting—in a word, phrase, or sentence(s); and (3) Thanksgiving—often with religious tones. Our text is an elaborate, highly religious form of the latter two parts of this manner of opening a letter. The salutation occurs in v. 4a (not in our reading); then, the greeting comes in vv. 4b-5a; and a complex thanksgiving fills out vv. 5b-8. The thanksgiving itself combines a polished doxology (vv. 5b-6), a prophetic word concerning the coming of Jesus Christ (v. 7), and a "word-of-God" in direct speech (v. 8).

Significance. It is difficult to imagine more doctrinal and confessional material being packed into four and a half verses of scripture than we find in this lesson. A careful look at the passage reveals themes and structures that are highly suggestive for proclamation.

First, the lectionary does not suggest reading v. 4a, but some awareness of the author and recipients is helpful for understanding the content of the following lines. The author is John, an early Christian leader who was exiled to the island of Patmos during a period of opposition or persecution of the Church in Asia Minor. The seven churches mentioned are named explicitly in a series of letters to the individual congregations in Revelation 2–3. Problems existed in these congregations because of the difficulties being experienced—suffering brought anxiety, doubts, and laxity.

Second, the greeting will seem familiar, for in a style similar to

Paul's, John pronounces "grace" and "peace" upon those reading Revelation. This grace and peace are specifically associated with God and Jesus Christ. Several items here merit attention. God is named in such a way that the reader ponders God's eternal character and majesty over all. Taken in the context of the whole of Revelation, however, these ascriptions are more than statements or recognitions of God's temporal infinity and omnipotence; these descriptions imply God's dependability and capacity to care for those in need. In turn, Jesus Christ is named in a three-fold ascription. He is called "faithful witness," a reference to his life and ministry, especially to his Passion and death. He is called "the firstborn of the dead," an unmistakable reference to his resurrection. And, he is called "the ruler of kings on earth," a recognition of his exaltation and Lordship. From this God and from this Jesus Christ, John speaks of grace and peace. Interpreters often explain that grace is the nature of God's saving work in Jesus Christ and that peace is the result of God's saving actions. In combinations with the ways John names God and Jesus Christ, we may also think of grace as God's nature or character and peace as God's goal in relation to humanity.

Third, the doxological pronouncements at the conclusion of the thanksgiving are more than lofty phrases heaped on the greeting like frosting on a cake. In the initial christological doxology we learn of the meaning of the work of Jesus Christ. The phrase "by his blood" indicates that John is offering an interpretation of the significance of the death of Jesus. It occurred for us out of Christ's love, and it gives us the freedom from our sins that grants us the peace that God desires for us. The statement is confessional, not explanatory. Moreover, the result of this freedom is that humanity is constituted as a "kingdom"—that is, the locus of the lordship of God, where God's will is supreme and John says those whom he addresses (Christians) are "priests"—that is, there is an equality in Christian faith that supersedes cultic ritual that distinguishes some persons as closer to God than others.

In turn, we hear of Jesus Christ's coming. The language of v. 7 employs words, phrases, and images related to the "day of the Lord," a day appointed by God on which the denizens of this world will be judged. As always in such eschatological passages, we are reminded that God through Christ rules the future, and the demand that God's standards regulate our lives is registered with force.

Finally, John reports God's own words. The phrase "Alpha and Omega" refer to the first and last letters of the Greek alphabet, so that God is "everything from A to Z." This inclusive "omni-image" refers back to the manner of naming God in the greeting (v. 4*b*) and even picks up the doxological language at the end of v. 6. The title applied here to God, "Almighty" *(pantocrator)*, recognizes that God is indeed Lord of all.

This compact, complex episolary opening informs John's readers (and us!) who God is, who Jesus Christ is, what God has done, is doing, and will do in Jesus Christ, and reminds them (and us!) that God's work in Jesus Christ places a claim on our lives. We are freed, but we are free for a purpose; and, God through Christ evaluates our lives. This declaration is more promise than threat, being meant to encourage those in difficulty to trust in God despite difficulties.

The Gospel: *John 18:33-37*

Jesus, the World, and the Truth

Setting. Commentators frequently refer to the second part of the Fourth Gospel (13:1–20:31) as "the book of glory," indicating this portion of the Gospel is the story of Jesus' glorification in fulfilling God's purposes. Chapter 13 recounts the last meal of Jesus with his disciples. Chapters 14–17 record Jesus' last discourse and his prayers for his disciples and all believers. Chapters 18–19 tell the story of Jesus' Passion, narrating the events of the Passion from the garden to the grave.

The Passion narrative in the gospel according to John is a unified, but elaborate, structure. There is a brief scene in the garden (18:1-12) followed by the blended scenes of Jesus before Annas (18:13-14, 19-24) and Peter in the courtyard of the high priest (18:15-18, 25-27). This leads to the lengthy trial before Pilate (18:28–19:16) which scholars regularly suggest unfolds in a series of seven scenes (18:28-32; 18:33-38*a*; 18:38*b*-40; 19:1-3; 19:4-8; 19:9-12*a*; and 19:12*b*-16). After this trial the story of Jesus being put to death is told in 19:17-37. The Passion narrative concludes with the account of

Jesus' burial (19:38-42). Our lesson comes from the second scene in the trial before Pilate.

Structure. The lesson simply recounts a conversation between Pilate and Jesus. The author seems removed from the scene, offering no commentary and few narrative phrases: Pilate asks Jesus a question; Jesus replies with a question; Pilate asks another question (or questions); Jesus answers directly but enigmatically nevertheless; Pilate asks another question; and Jesus answers, again directly but speaking in typical Johannine metaphors. The lesson omits the final element of the conversation, the well-known question by Pilate, "What is truth?" Without this memorable query, the two statements by Jesus in vv. 36 and 37 are the dominant elements of conversation. In essence, three related points are made: (1) Jesus' kingdom is not of this world. (2) He came into the world to testify to the truth. (3) Persons of truth heed Jesus' voice.

Significance. Pilate demonstrates awareness of the charge against Jesus when he poses his opening question. In his mouth, the question of Jesus' identity as King of the Jews can only have a political cast; we see no evidence that Pilate was interested in the religious matter of blasphemy. In contrast to the Synoptic Gospels, Jesus' reply to Pilate is an explanation. Matthew, Mark, and Luke have Jesus merely reply to the question with a cryptic Greek sentence that is usually translated, "You say so." Commentators suggest that Jesus' answer in the Synoptics is a way of saying that what Pilate suggests is correct, but Jesus himself does not understand kingship in the same way that Pilate does. Actually the line in the Synoptics literally says, "You yourself say," or, to paraphrase, "You tell me." In John, however, the issue of Jesus' kingship is not so open to interpretation and misinterpretation, because John has Jesus offer a careful, though still enigmatic, explanation of his kingdom. Quite clearly Jesus' kingdom is not political, rather it is religious. Yet, we should also recognize that Jesus' statement that his kingdom is not "of" this world indicates that his religious kingdom does not originate in this world, but with God.

Jews traditionally understood that God was the King of Israel, no matter who sat upon an earthly throne. Even when David was King, he was but God's regent. Jesus' declarations reveal the religious nature of his kingdom and declare the religious sense of his kingship. Were he a political king, there would have been political followers ready to fight for his recognition, but there were no such defenders, because his kingdom and his kingship are religious. Jesus plainly states that he came into the world "to testify to the truth"—that is, to the kingship of God. Thus, Jesus presents himself as God's regent, though unlike others because of his heavenly origin. Jesus' mission was to declare God's truth (ultimate kingship) and to assemble God's own people (everyone who belongs to the truth).

Pilate never seems to understand. His questions throughout this conversation (including v. 38a) come more out of curiosity than cynicism and demonstrate his lack of comprehension. But, readers of John know that Jesus came into the world to call God's people by speaking the truth of God, including especially the magnitude of God's love revealed in Jesus himself. This revelation, however, brings the crisis of separation of those on the side of the truth (God) from those on the side of the world (the Devil).

Proper 29: The Celebration

Today is the last Sunday in the Christian year, the Festival of Christ the King or the Reign of Christ. The Old Testament lesson brings us back to a consideration of David, who has figured largely in the post-Pentecost readings this year. We hear him uttering words of promise and of judgment—judgment upon the rulers of this world limited by their godlessness and lack of apprehension of the truth (Pilate in the Gospel lesson), and a divine promise, realized in the elder John's vision on Patmos, that God will be everlastingly faithful to the covenant.

There will be cultural pressures in many churches to make this "Thanksgiving Sunday" and to avoid the questions raised by today's lessons. To the degree that the Thanksgiving emphasis is purely an exercise in patriotic triumphalism, the lessons may be antidotal. David's oracle suggests qualities appropriate for national life: Is our administration of justice an occasion for thanksgiving for those who are subject to it? Is the object of our thanksgiving our own greed and self-satisfaction, or does our thanksgiving grow out of knowing who

163

Christ is (the faithful witness, the firstborn of the dead, the ruler of the kings of the earth) and who we are (a priestly kingdom called into being by our participation in the death of Christ)?

Two well-known hymns based in part on the Revelation lesson are "Lo, He Comes with Clouds Descending," and "Mine Eyes Have Seen the Glory."

The following Wesley stanza, sung to the tune Easter with the alleluia after each line, can serve as a response to the second lesson:

> He has our salvation wrought,
> He our captive souls has bought,
> He has reconciled to God,
> He has washed us in [freed us by] his blood.

The alternative in the last line will depend upon which translation is used in the reading. The use of the familiar Easter tune is not only because it is familiar, but to remind us through the music as we complete another cycle of the Christian year that this celebration of Christ the King is the result of the Easter triumph and consequent upon it, that all of our liturgy is a commentary on the Paschal mystery. Jesus, as the second lesson says, is the firstborn of the dead.

The Gospel lesson makes clear the unique and revolutionary character of the kingship of Christ. The "ruler of the kings of the earth" (Revelation) rules from the throne of the cross, and so provides the model for those of us who witness to him. An appropriate visual for today would be the *Christus Rex,* a form of the cross which shows Christ upon it, but clothed in priestly and/or royal garb. This will help symbolize the paradox of the Servant King.

Thanksgiving Day

Old Testament Texts

Joel 2:21-27 describes how God's actions on the Day of the Lord can change their direction or goal in light of Israel's response to prophetic judgment. Psalm 126 is a poem about Israel's reversal of fortune.

The Lesson: *Joel 2:21-27*

Petition and Assurance

Setting. The reference to the Day of the Lord in Joel 2:1 provides important background for interpreting the Old Testament lesson. The Day of the Lord is not a twenty-four hour period of time. In fact, it is not a definite period of time at all. A better way of thinking about the Day of the Lord is to associate it with a definite divine event in time. The definite event is an action by God that determines the character of the world. The Exodus is such an event, or, in the New Testament, the mission of Jesus. Such actions are God's Day, and because the events reshape our world, there is always a present quality to them.

The Day of the Lord was Israel's way of describing how God breaks into our world in special ways to bring about a new salvation. Scholars debate the particular setting in which the term *Day of the Lord* was first used. It may have been in the context of holy war when Israel saw that real security was not rooted in their military strength but in God. In this context the *Day of the Lord* was a confession that only the wrath of God could really defeat Israel's enemies. Thus military victory was interpreted as the Day of the Lord, and its celebration required worship because God's defeat of threatening nations embodied the essence of what salvation meant. Over time the Day of the Lord became one of the central events in Israel's worship, where it was symbolized as bright light. Israel lived for the Day of the Lord. A close analogy in Christian tradition would be an Easter sunrise service, where the light from the rising sun also symbolizes salvation.

Many prophetic oracles presuppose this powerful tradition of salvation in Israel's ongoing worship, in order to confront the people of God with their own sin. The Day of the Lord, therefore, is frequently used as a reversal—as a dark and gloomy day of judgment for the people of God rather than the nations. Amos 5:18 provides an early example of this reversal. Here the prophet presents a judgment oracle by stating: "Woe to you who desire the day of the Lord! Why would you have the day of the Lord? It is darkness, and not light." Joel 2:1-2, 12-17 is a prophetic oracle in the tradition of Amos, where the prophet uses a strong tradition of salvation to declare judgment on the people of God for not living out God's salvation. Simply put, the judgment is that God has declared holy war on his own people. But Israel can influence the direction of God's holy war by how they respond to the threat. Because of this fact, Joel 2:21-27 presents a reversal within a reversal, in which God changes direction in order to save rather than destroy Israel in light of their cultic acts of repentance.

Structure. Joel 2:21-27 must be read in the larger context of vv. 18-27, which, in turn, must be interpreted in an even larger context of Israel's cultic acts of repentance in v. 17. The prophetic threat of the inevitable Day of the Lord in 2:1-11 led to the proper response of repentance in v. 17, which now elicits a change of direction in God's action toward Israel. Instead of destroying, God becomes jealous for Israel (v. 18). Verse 18 provides an introductory statement about a changed state of affairs in God, which is followed by three divine statements of assurance in vv. 19-20, 21-24, 25-27. The context of reversal is important for preaching Joel 2:21-27, yet there is no clue of this reversal if the text is limited to vv. 21-27. Consequently, the preacher may wish either to expand the boundaries of the text or to provide the necessary background at the time of reading or preaching.

Significance. Verses 19-20 provide the initial divine response to Israel's plea for forgiveness and for rescue from the judgment of the Day of the Lord. Note how v. 19 reads, "In response to his people the LORD said." The response is in two parts: God will replenish the earth, and thus reverse the drought and locust plagues described in chapter 1 and God will reverse the mythological judgment of the Day itself, which is symbolized by the imagery of the foe from the north. The lectionary text focuses on the first response by describing how God will replenish the earth for Israel rather than destroy it. This focus on the earth and its bounty as divine gift to Israel is certainly the reason why this text has been picked for Thanksgiving.

Two oracles about the earth follow in vv. 21-24 and 25-27. Both represent reversals from images of judgment in chapter 1. Verses 21-24 describe how the drought of 1:16-20 will be reversed by repeating the specific motifs of animals, pastures, produce, and rain (rather than drought). The reason for the reversal is stated in v. 23. It is literally "food or early rain for righteousness" (Hebrew, *hammoreh lisdakah;* NRSV translates less clearly, "early rain for your vindication"). Verses 25-27 describe how the locust plague of 1:4 will be reversed. This unit ends with the recognition formula in v. 27 that Israel will know God. Verse 27 provides the point of focus for preaching this text, for it brings the cycle of judgment (Joel 1:1–2:11) and its reversal (2:18-27) full circle. In the face of judgment Israel pleaded for God's relief, to which God responded by reversing both the plague and locust and the drought, which were seen as signs that the Day of the Lord was now an event of judgment for Israel. Their reversal is an indication of a new salvation for Israel, which is imaged in a renewed and abundant land. The meaning of vv. 21-27, however, is not limited to the reversal of drought and plague to a plentiful harvest. Rather the reversals signified in the bountiful land must be accompanied by Israel's recognition of God in the midst of the harvest, and that the divine presence is the result of God's changed action toward the people and the land. It is the food or early rain for righteousness. Here lies the groundwork for celebrating Thanksgiving.

The Response: *Psalm 126*

Petition and Assurance

Setting. Psalm 126 is about a reversal of fortune, which makes it a particularly appropriate response to Joel 2:21-27. Two reversals are referred to in vv. 1-3 and in v. 4. Verses 1-3 describe the reversal of fortune for Zion, while v. 4 focuses on the worshiping community. Ambiguity concerning the temporal relationship between these two points of focus yields two different interpretations of the psalm.

Structure. Psalm 126 can be separated into two or three parts. Verses 1-3 focus on Zion, v. 4 is a petition by the community, and vv. 5-6 present words of promise or confidence.

Significance. Scholars separate on whether the restoration of Zion in vv. 1-3 should be read as a future or as a past event. Thus, is the psalm eschatological in its orientation or a reflection on history? If the psalm is read as a future hope, then the petition in v. 4 is a plea for the realization of vv. 1-3 and vv. 5-6 function as prophetic promise. If the psalm is read as a reflection on a past event then v. 4 is a more specific plea that the people be restored along with Zion or it is a petition of renewal, to which vv. 5-6 become a statement of confidence. This ambiguity invites the preacher or worship leader to determine the appropriate reading of the psalm for each specific community.

New Testament Texts

The lessons for Thanksgiving are a pair of exhortations which actually instruct believers about the proper objects of prayer and the proper disposition and course of life. These texts work well together in relation to the general idea of giving thanks, and more importantly, both readings contain pointed theological statements. A Thanksgiving meditation or sermon may well touch on the themes inherent in both texts, and by attending to the theological contents of both lessons the proclamation will find genuine Christian content that ensures a message that is more than a generic call to gratitude for all that is good in life.

The Epistle: *I Timothy 2:1-7*

Praying for the Right Things

Setting. The opening chapter of I Timothy establishes the occasion for the letter, revealing that there are false teachers whose work and teaching are to be opposed by those with correct theological sensibilities and correspondingly pure lives. After the first chapter, the epistle continues by offering a set of pointed directions in 2:1–3:13. Commentators regularly refer to 2:1–3:13 as a small church manual. The first distinguishable unit of guidelines in this larger section is our epistle lesson. These verses are a statement about prayer, and they are concerned with the objects of prayer and with the theological basis of appropriate praying. Further teaching about prayer, essentially declaring what is proper deportment in prayer, comes in 2:8-15. After these two sections on praying, I Timothy treats the qualification of church leaders and, then, returns to the issue of false teachers.

Structure. One clear thread runs through this whole paragraph and holds it together—namely, the author's regularly repeated conviction that the gospel and the life of Christian faith are concerned with all human beings (see vv. 1, 4, and 6). This unifying interest, however, should not obscure the motion of the author's thought in these verses. First, the author calls for prayer for everyone (v. 1). Second, he digresses momentarily to focus the need for prayer specifically in relation to leaders of all kinds; yet, even this prayer is for the well-being of all (v. 2). Third, in vv. 3-4 we find that such prayer is pleasing to God, and we learn that the God who accepts such praying is the one who desires for all persons to be saved and to know the truth. Fourth, this theological verification of the call to prayer for all persons is itself validated by the inclusion of what interpreters judge to be a creedal statement in vv. 5-6. And, fifth, we learn that the apostle Paul was appointed to instruct the Gentiles in matters of faith and truth because of God's concern for the welfare of all humans (v. 7).

Significance. In a nutshell, this lesson is a call to prayer for a life of peace and godliness for all humanity as they are established in faith and the truth according to the will of God made known and active by and through Jesus Christ and, now, in the continuing ministry of the apostle. This is a large, complex, but single idea.

Above all, what Christians have to be thankful for is that God wills and works for the salvation of all persons. Salvation means that because of what God has done in Jesus Christ (the message born by the Church to the rest of the world) humans are being brought to faith and to a knowledge of God's truth. The result of the advent of faith and truth in the lives of humans is that their manner of life is transformed. Persons of faith and truth lead respectable, godly, peaceful lives. This means that order is restored to human existence as humans are brought together under the saving grace of Jesus Christ. This harmony among humans is genuinely expressive of the oneness of God, who through Jesus Christ has grasped a once fragmented humanity and brought them together with himself into the context of the new community of faith.

Those who experience and know this saving work of God through Jesus Christ find their lives transformed. And as they orient themselves toward God through prayer, they offer God thanks for what has been done and is being done for others (and themselves). A true prayer combining petition and thanksgiving will always tend toward praise and asking God to do more of what has been done rather than toward telling God how to be as good as we would be if we were God.

Implicit in this lesson is a denunciation of disorder and particularity that denies and undermines the universal scope of God's concern with all humankind (a stance typical of the false teachers already criticized in chapter 1, and who will be criticized further in the latter portions of the letter). The one God is the God of all, and in Jesus Christ God acts to reunite humans with one another as through Christ they are reunited with God. For this we give God thanks in prayer.

The Gospel: *Matthew 6:25-33*

Seek First the Kingdom and God's Righteousness

Setting. For the second time during Year B we encounter a text from Matthew's Sermon on the Mount. This lesson calls us away from unnecessary anxiety over the needs of daily life to a complete concern with God's kingdom and righteousness. The call away from anxiety makes this an appropriate text for Thanksgiving, and the call to giving top priority to God's will and ways distinguishes our thanksgiving as genuinely Christian gratitude.

Commentators recognize Matthew 5–7 as the full Sermon, and within the whole collection of Jesus' teaching they recognize subunits that are highly organized and deliberately set in balanced structure. The larger section within which our lesson occurs is 6:19–7:11, a collection of sayings set in balance with 5:21-48 in the total Sermon (both contain fifty-nine lines in Greek).

Structure. The verses of our lesson are held together by various key words that run through nearly every line of the unit. The material is a sequence of prohibitions and imperatives that function more as commandments than suggestions. The lesson opens with a bold prohibition against being senselessly concerned with life (v. 25a). In support of this prohibition we find a complex series of rhetorical questions and illustrations from life (vv. 25b-30). A second prohibition returns directly to the theme of senseless concern (v. 31); one further illustration of the theme is given (v. 32a), but merely as a bridge to a blunt statement of why senseless concern is unnecessary (v. 32b). Next, an imperative directs the readers/hearers to positive action (v. 33a) and a promise is made for the obedient (v. 33b). A wisdom maxim completes the unit (v. 34).

Significance. This lesson seems to need a defender. The simple, naive piety of the sayings has drawn especially harsh criticism through the ages. Dying birds (not to mention other animals and humans) caught in the tragedy of famine conditions and even the ravages of war-torn regions contradict the claims of the senselessness of concern with life's necessities. The text seeks to draw our attention away from worry and involvement with mundane needs to the seemingly higher care for religious and moral matters. But one shame of the centuries is that this call to God's kingdom and righteousness is regularly cited as a defense of plain old laziness. Indeed, the text can even be taken as a denunciation of prudence. And so, commentators regularly leap to defend these words of Jesus, suggesting that Jesus is not talking economics or a work ethic, but rather religion and morality.

Nevertheless, as people have pondered Jesus' declarations through the centuries, many have been troubled and even offended by his words.

Two issues are crucial for the interpretation of this lesson. First, what is the text referring to when it advises against "concern" and "care"? Is Jesus a happy-go-lucky, "don't worry be happy" type? Is he commanding us not to be greedy? Is he telling us not to be slaves to anxiety, especially over material goods? Is he talking about our essential attitude, which issues in our actions? Second, to whom is this teaching addressed? Is Jesus speaking to all pious persons or to his disciples doing ministry or to the poor or to the rich? We shall work backwards through these issues.

Verses 31-33 indicate that Jesus' words are not addressed to pious persons in general, for they frame the issue of concern with the necessities of life along ethnic lines that indicate that Jesus is speaking to specific persons. The persons addressed are those familiar with the concepts of the kingdom, God's righteousness, and God as heavenly Father. This combination indicates that Jesus offered these explicit commands to the members of the community he called together in the course of his ministry. This would include his disciples, but the assembly portrayed at the outset of the Sermon is broader than the disciples alone. Nevertheless, since the teaching of Jesus was preserved by the early Christian community, we can understand that it was in the Church that this teaching had particular meaning, so that Jesus' commandments in Matthew are directed toward shaping the life of the Church.

Jesus' words about not caring or being concerned with the necessities of life is a radical call to life itself. Jesus' commandment forbids both inactive anxiety and anxious active attempts to secure life through things. The call is disturbing, and it is formulated and repeated in a way that shows it is meant to be so. This is not a call away from common sense and basic prudence, rather it is a call away from an attempt to secure life through human effort, especially in terms of material goods. This is a call to God and godliness—to trust God and therefore to have a godly existence. Jesus calls the Church to relate to God and to form life out of that relationship. The reality of the relationship is assumed, but our experiencing freedom by living toward God is not. In other words, we can obey or disobey Jesus.

Thanksgiving Day: The Celebration

The epistle lesson calls our attention to the importance of offering prayers and thanksgivings for everyone as part of our Christian duty. This raises the question of how the work of prayer is performed in the Christian assembly.

The classical pattern divides prayer into five types: adoration, confession of sin, intercession, petition, and thanksgiving. Attention should be paid to see that these categories are properly represented over time in a congregation's liturgical offering. They need not be equally represented each week. Greater attention to confession may be more appropriate during Advent and Lent than during Christmas and Eastertide.

Adoration and thanksgiving are frequently confused. Adoration is the praise of God for being God; it is being lost "in wonder, love, and praise" for no other reason than that God is! Thanksgiving refers to what God has done for us in creating, redeeming, and sustaining us, "for our creation, redemption, and all the blessings of this life," as the old General Thanksgiving put it. All too often prayers of thanksgiving remain localized and we forget to thank God for the blessings that others have received.

Intercession and petition are also frequently confused. Intercessions are for others; petitions are for ourselves. Again, in local churches where the old pastoral prayer has given way to a sharing of joys and concerns, care needs to be taken to see that petitions do not crowd out the intercessions.

Public sharing of prayer concerns in the congregation is one way for the people to practice the priesthood that is theirs by baptism, but it must be remembered that a priest's primary function is to intercede for others. The English word *pontifical*, which now relates to bishops, in its origin comes from a Latin word for priest, *pontifex*, which means "a bridge builder." In prayer we build bridges between God and the world.

The practice of sharing joys and concerns in no way absolves the pastor of the responsibility for overseeing the whole work of prayer and maintaining a proper balance between the five categories. If the people's intercessions have not gotten beyond the walls of the local church, it is the pastor's job to bid their prayers for wider intentions. A practice sometimes seen in local churches, and which should be discouraged, is to have the pastor list the intentions raised during the sharing and then repeat them all over again in a pastoral prayer. This is an exercise in sacerdotalism, which denies the priestly character of the baptized and implies that all prayer needs to have a clerical rubber stamp. Usually in such cases, by the time the pastor has repeated the earlier intentions, there is no time to raise the neglected items for which the pastor should be responsible.

Prayers of thanksgiving on this day should be general in scope while not denying persons the opportunity to express individual thanks. Litanies of thanksgiving may be found in the *The New Handbook of the Christian Year* (Abingdon Press, 1992), pp. 272-73 and *The Worshipbook* (Presbyterian, 1970), pp. 114-15. A large collection of prayers of thanksgiving is in the *Book of Common Prayer*, pp. 836-41.

Scripture Index

Old Testament

Genesis
2..85
12..145
14..85

Exodus
4:25...135

Numbers
14..85

Deuteronomy
24......................................77, 78
25:5-10...................................135

Judges
3:24...135

Ruth
1:1..115
1:1-18....................................114-17
3:1-5.....................................134-36
4:13-17..................................134, 135
4:13-22....................................115
4:14...137

I Samuel
1:4-20...................................144-46
1:21-28....................................146
2:1-10..................................146, 147
2:9-11.......................................154
21:25..152
24:3...135

II Samuel
22:2–23:7.................................154
23:1-7..................................154-56

Esther
4:14...61
6:13...61
7:1-6, 9-10............................59, 60
8:3-8..62
9:20-22..................................59, 60

Job
1–2.......................................80, 92
1:1, 2:1-10.............................69-73
1:6-22..70
1:8, 2:3......................................95
2:11-13......................................70
3–14..81
3–27.....................................80, 81
3–37..92
8–10..81
11–14..81
15–21..81
22.....................................82-84, 94
23:1-9, 16-17.........................80-85
26:8-12......................................95
32–37..80
38...94
38:1-7, 34-41............................92
38:4-7..95
38:8-11......................................95
38–41..................................92, 105
40:3-5..93
42:1-6, 10-17..........................103-6

Psalms
1..41, 52
2...98
19......................................41-43

Psalms—cont.
22:1-15................................85
24.....................................128
26................................73, 74
34:1-8, 19-22........................107
34:11-22.............................107
45:1-2, 6-9......................21, 22
45:10-17............................. 22
95......................................85
104....................................92
104:1-9, 24, 35...................... 96
110................................ 85, 98
124....................................62
125.............................. 32, 33
126................................. 168
127.......................... 136, 137
131:1-18................ 154, 157, 158
132.................................. 158
146............................. 114, 117
146–150.............................. 117

Proverbs
1–9............................ 30, 40, 41
1:20-33............................39-41
9:1-6......................... 39, 41, 50
10:1–22:16.......................... 30
22:1-2, 8-9, 22-23................29-31
22:17–24:22........................30
24:23-34............................ 30
25–29...............................30
30:1-9.............................. 30
30:10-33............................ 30
31:1-9.............................. 30
31:1-33.............................49
31:10-31..................... 30, 49-51

Song of Songs
2:8-13............................. 19, 20

Isaiah
24–27............................... 125
25:6-9............................124-28

Joel
2:1-2, 12-17.......................... 166
2:19-20.......................166, 167
2:21-27.......................... 165-68

New Testament

Matthew
5–7.................................. 171
6:19–7:11............................ 171
6:25-33......................170, 172
12:30................................ 65
15:21-31............................. 35

Mark
7:1-8, 14-15, 21-23............. 25, 26
7:24-37.............................35, 36
8:22–10:52......................... 45
8:27-38............................45, 46
8:31–9:30............................45
9:30-37.............................54, 55
9:31–10:32......................... 45
9:38-50.............................65, 66
9:38–10:31......................... 65
10:2-16............................76, 77
10:17-31............................ 87-89
10:35-45................... 45, 99, 100
10:46-52...................... 110, 111
11:1–12:44..........................120
12:28-34................... 120, 121
12:31.............................. 34
13:1-8...................... 150, 151
11:1–12:44.........................139
12:38-44......................139-41
14–16.............................. 150
14:50.............................102

John
11:1-5...............................131
11:1-54............................ 130
11:6-16..............................131
11:17-27............................131
11:28-32............................131
11:32-44.......................130-32
11:33-41............................131
11:41-44............................131
11:45-54............................131
13:1–20:31.........................161
18–19..............................161
18:1-12.............................161
18:13-14............................161
18:15-18, 25-27.....................161

John—cont.
18:28–19:16........................ 161
18:33-37....................... 161, 162
19:17-37.............................161
19:38-42.............................161

Acts
13:33................................. 51

I Timothy
2:1-7.............................169, 170
2:1–3:13............................. 169
2:8-15...............................169

Hebrews
1:1-4, 2:5-12.....................74, 75
2:9................................. 79
3:1................................... 85
4:12-16..............................85
4:14–7:28........ 85-87, 97, 108, 109
5:1-10............................... 97
7:23-28............................ 108
8:1–10:18......................118, 148
8:1–10:25........................... 148

Hebrews—cont.
9:11-14..........................118, 119
9:22-23.............................. 120
9:24-28......................... 137-39
10:11-14, 15-18, 25..........148, 149
10:19–12:29......................... 148

James
1:1..................................... 23
1:2-16................................ 23
1:17-27............................23, 24
1:19-20...............................43
1:26..................................43
2:1-16................................ 23
2:1-17........................... 33, 34
2:1–3:12......................... 33, 52
3:1-12............................43, 44
3:13-20............................63, 64
5:13-20............................63, 64

Revelation
1:4-8............................. 158-61
19:1–22:5........................... 129
21:1-6.............................128-30

A Comparison of Major Lectionaries

YEAR B: PROPERS 17 THROUGH 29 AND ALL SAINTS AND THANKSGIVING DAYS

	Old Testament	Psalm	Epistle	Gospel
PROPER 17 (August 28–September 3)				
	[RC: 22nd Ordinary Time]		[Luth: 15th After Pentecost]	
RCL	Song Sol. 2:8-13	45:1-2, 6-9	James 1:17-27	Mark 7:1-8, 14-15, 21-23
RoCath	Deut. 4:1-2, 6-8	15:2-5	James 1:17-18, 21-22, 27	
Episcopal	Deut. 4:1-9	15	Eph. 6:10-20	
Lutheran	Deut. 4:1-2, 6-8		Eph. 6:10-20	
PROPER 18 (September 4-10)				
	[RC: 23rd Ordinary Time]		[Luth: 16th After Pentecost]	
RCL	Prov. 22:1-2, 8-9, 22-23	125	James 2:1-10 (11-13), 14-17	Mark 7:24-37
RoCath	Isa. 35:4-7	146:7-10	James 2:1-5	Mark 7:31-37
Episcopal	Isa. 35:4-7a	146	James 1:17-27	Mark 7:31-37
Lutheran	Isa. 35:4-7a	146	James 1:17-27	Mark 7:31-37

	Old Testament	Psalm	Epistle	Gospel
PROPER 19 (September 11-17)				
	[RC: 24th Ordinary Time]		[Luth: 17th After Pentecost]	
RCL	Prov. 1:20-33	19	James 3:1-12	Mark 8:27-38
RoCath	Isa. 50:4-9	116:1-6, 8-9	James 2:14-18	Mark 8:27-35
Episcopal	Isa. 50:4-9	116	James 2:1-5, 8-10, 14-18	
Lutheran	Isa. 50:4-10	116:1-8	James 2:1-5, 8-10, 14-18	Mark 8:27-35
PROPER 20 (September 18-24)				
	[RC: 25th Ordinary Time]		[Luth: 18th After Pentecost]	
RCL	Prov. 31:10-31	1	James 3:13-4:3, 7-8a	Mark 9:30-37
RoCath	Wis. 2:17-20	54:3-8	James 3:16-4:3	
Episcopal	Wis. 1:16-2:1 (16-11) 12-22	54	James 3:16-4:6	
Lutheran	Jer. 11:18-20	54:1-4, 6-7a	James 3:16-4:6	

	Old Testament	Psalm	Epistle	Gospel
PROPER 21 (September 25–October 1)				
	[RC: 26th Ordinary Time]		[Luth: 19th After Pentecost]	
RCL	Esther 7:1-6, 9-10; 9:20-22	124	James 5:13-20	Mark 9:38-50
RoCath	Num. 11:25-29	19:8, 10, 12-14	James 5:1-6	Mark 9:38-43, 45, 47-48
Episcopal	Num. 11:4-6, 10-16, 24-29	19	James 4:7–5:6	Mark 9:38-43, 45, 47-48
Lutheran	Num. 11:4-6, 10-16, 24-29	135:1-7, 13-14	James 4:7–5:6	
PROPER 22 (October 2-8)				
	[RC: 27th Ordinary Time]		[Luth: 20th After Pentecost]	
RCL	Job 1:1; 2:1-10	26	Heb. 1:1-4; 2:5-12	Mark 10:2-16
RoCath	Gen. 2:18-24	128:1-6	Heb. 2:9-11	
Episcopal	Gen. 2:18-24	8	Heb. 2:1-18	Mark 10:2-9
Lutheran	Gen. 2:18-24	128	Heb. 2:9-18	

	Old Testament	Psalm	Epistle	Gospel

PROPER 23 (October 9-15)
[RC: 28th Ordinary Time]   [Luth: 21st After Pentecost]

	Old Testament	Psalm	Epistle	Gospel
RCL	Job 23:1-9, 16-17	22:1-15	Heb. 4:12-16	Mark 10:17-31
RoCath	Wis. 7:7-10	90:12-17	Heb. 4:12-13	Mark 10:17-30
Episcopal	Amos 5:6-7, 10-15	90	Heb. 3:1-6	
Lutheran	Amos 5:6-7, 10-15	90:12-17	Heb. 3:1-6	

PROPER 24 (October 16-22)
[RC: 29th Ordinary Time]   [Luth: 22nd After Pentecost]

	Old Testament	Psalm	Epistle	Gospel
RCL	Job 38:1-7 (34-41)	104:1-9, 24, 35c	Heb. 5:1-10	Mark 10:35-45
RoCath	Isa. 53:10-11	33:4-5, 18-20, 22	Heb. 4:14-16	
Episcopal	Isa. 53:4-12	91	Heb. 4:12-16	
Lutheran	Isa. 53:10-12	91:9-16	Heb. 4:9-16	

	Old Testament	Psalm	Epistle	Gospel

PROPER 25 (October 23-29)

[RC: 30th Ordinary Time] [Luth: 23rd After Pentecost]

	Old Testament	Psalm	Epistle	Gospel
RCL	Job 42:1-6, 10-17	34:1-8 (19-22)	Heb. 7:23-28	Mark 10:46-52
RoCath	Jer. 31:7-9	126:1-6	Heb. 5:1-6	
Episcopal	Isa. 59:(1-4) 9-19)	13	Heb. 5:12–6:1, 9-12	
Lutheran	Jer. 31:7-9	126	Heb. 5:1-10	

PROPER 26 (October 30–November 5)

[RC: 31st Ordinary Time] [Luth: 24th After Pentecost]

	Old Testament	Psalm	Epistle	Gospel
RCL	Ruth 1:1-18	146	Heb. 9:11-14	Mark 12:28-34
RoCath	Deut. 6:2-6	18:2-4, 47, 51	Heb. 7:23-28	
Episcopal	Deut. 6:1-9	119:1-16	Heb. 7:23-28	
Lutheran	Deut. 6:1-9	119:1-16	Heb. 7:23-28	Mark 12:28-34 (35-37)

	Old Testament	Psalm	Epistle	Gospel

PROPER 27 (November 6-12)

[RC: 32nd Ordinary Time]   [Luth: 25th After Pentecost]

	Old Testament	Psalm	Epistle	Gospel
RCL	Ruth 3:1-5, 4:13-17	127	Heb. 9:24-28	Mark 12:38-44
RoCath	I Kings 17:10-16	146:7-10		
Episcopal	I Kings 17:8-16	146		
Lutheran	I Kings 17:8-16	107:1-3, 33-43		Mark 12:41-44

PROPER 28 (November 13-19)

[RC: 33rd Ordinary Time]   [Luth: 26th After Pentecost]

	Old Testament	Psalm	Epistle	Gospel
RCL	I Sam. 1:4-20	I Sam. 2:1-10	Heb. 10:11-14 (15-18), 19-25	Mark 13:1-8
RoCath	Dan. 12:1-3	16:5, 8-11	Heb. 10:11-14, 18	Mark 13:24-32
Episcopal	Dan. 12:1-4a (5-13)	16	Heb. 10:31-39	Mark 13:14-23
Lutheran	Dan. 12:1-3	16	Heb. 10:11-18	Mark 13:1-13

CHRIST THE KING OR REIGN OF CHRIST SUNDAY
PROPER 29 (November 20-26)
[RC: 34th Ordinary Time] [Luth: Last After Pentecost]

	Old Testament	Psalm	Epistle	Gospel
RCL	II Sam. 23:1-7	132:1-12 (13-18)	Rev. 1:4*b*-8	John 18:33-37
RoCath	Dan. 7:13-14	93:1-2, 5	Rev. 1:5-8	
Episcopal	Dan. 7:9-14	93	Rev. 1:1-8	
Lutheran	Dan. 7:13-14	93		

ALL SAINTS DAY

	Old Testament	Psalm	Epistle	Gospel
RCL	Isa. 25:6-9	24	Rev. 21:1-6*a*	John 11:32-44
RoCath	Rev. 7:2-4, 9-14	24:1-6	I John 3:1-3	Matt. 5:1-12
Episcopal	Sir. 44:1-10, 13-14	149	Rev. 7:2-4, 9-17	Matt. 5:1-12
Lutheran	Isa. 26:1-4, 8-9, 12-13, 19-21	34:1-10	Rev. 21:9-11, 22-27 (22:1-5)	Matt. 5:1-12

THANKSGIVING DAY

	Old Testament	Psalm	Epistle	Gospel
RCL	Joel 2:21-27	126	I Tim. 2:1-7	Matt. 6:25-33
RoCath	Isa. 63:7-9	113:1-8	Eph. 1:3-14	Mark 5:18-20
Episcopal	Deut. 8:1-3, 6-10 (17-20)	65	James 1:17-18, 21-27	
Lutheran	Deut. 8:1-10	65	I Tim. 2:1-4	Luke 17:11-19

A Liturgical Calendar

September Through Christ the King 1993–2001

	1993 A	1994 B	1995 C	1996 A	1997 B
Proper 17	Aug. 29	Aug. 28	Sept. 3	Sept. 1	Aug. 31
Proper 18	Sept. 5	Sept. 4	Sept. 10	Sept. 8	Sept. 7
Proper 19	Sept. 12	Sept. 11	Sept. 17	Sept. 15	Sept. 14
Proper 20	Sept. 19	Sept. 18	Sept. 24	Sept. 22	Sept. 21
Proper 21	Sept. 26	Sept. 25	Oct. 1	Sept. 29	Sept. 28
Proper 22	Oct. 3	Oct. 2	Oct. 8	Oct. 6	Oct. 5
Proper 23	Oct. 10	Oct. 9	Oct. 15	Oct. 13	Oct. 12
Proper 24	Oct. 17	Oct. 16	Oct. 22	Oct. 20	Oct. 19
Proper 25	Oct. 24	Oct. 23	Oct. 29	Oct. 27	Oct. 26
Proper 26	Oct. 31	Oct. 30	Nov. 5	Nov. 3	Nov. 2
Proper 27	Nov. 7	Nov. 6	Nov. 12	Nov. 10	Nov. 9
Proper 28	Nov. 14	Nov. 13	Nov. 19	Nov. 17	Nov. 16
Proper 29	Nov. 21	Nov. 20	Nov. 26	Nov. 24	Nov. 23
(Christ the King)					

	1998 C	1999 A	2000 B	2001 C
Proper 17	Aug. 30	Aug. 29	Sept. 3	Sept. 2
Proper 18	Sept. 6	Sept. 5	Sept. 10	Sept. 9
Proper 19	Sept. 13	Sept. 12	Sept. 17	Sept. 16
Proper 20	Sept. 20	Sept. 19	Sept. 24	Sept. 23
Proper 21	Sept. 27	Sept. 26	Oct. 1	Sept. 30
Proper 22	Oct. 4	Oct. 3	Oct. 8	Oct. 7
Proper 23	Oct. 11	Oct. 10	Oct. 15	Oct. 14
Proper 24	Oct. 18	Oct. 17	Oct. 22	Oct. 21
Proper 25	Oct. 25	Oct. 24	Oct. 29	Oct. 28
Proper 26	Nov. 1	Oct. 31	Nov. 5	Nov. 4
Proper 27	Nov. 8	Nov. 7	Nov. 12	Nov. 11
Proper 28	Nov. 15	Nov. 14	Nov. 19	Nov. 18
Proper 29	Nov. 22	Nov. 21	Nov. 26	Nov. 25

(Christ the King)